MW01616231

A
HOUSE
DIVIDED

Technology, Worship, and
Healing the Church After COVID

BENJAMIN D. GIFFONE

Copyright © 2025 by Benjamin D. Giffone

Published by the Libertarian Christian Institute Press

Cover design and typesetting by Nicole Sturk. Artwork
copyright Ethan Magness. Used with Permission.

ISBN: 978-1-7336584-7-8

Unless otherwise noted, scripture quotations are from the ESV® Bible
(The Holy Bible, English Standard Version®), © 2001 by Crossway,
a publishing ministry of Good News Publishers. Used by permission.
All rights reserved. The ESV text may not be quoted in any publication
made available to the public by a Creative Commons license. The ESV
may not be translated in whole or in part into any other language.

To Dainius, Deivydas, Lisa, Modestas, Raimondas, and Susan:
diverse backgrounds and differing views, but one in Christ.

———————————

"...God is really among you!"

(1 COR 14:25)

Also by Benjamin D. Giffone

*My Salvation Is Close At Hand: Isaiah 56–66
for the Church After Christendom*

*Storymaking, Textual Development, and Varying Cultic
Centralizations: Gathering and Fitting Unhewn Stones*

*Sit at My Right Hand: The Chronicler's Portrait of the
Tribe of Benjamin in the Social Context of Yehud*

*Economics Before Economics: Chapters of History of
Economic Thought before Adam Smith* (co-authored
with Tomáš Evan and Jonathan Warner)

Also by The Libertarian Christian Institute

*Faith Seeking Freedom: Libertarian Christian
Answers to Tough Questions*

*Strangers with Candy: Observations from the
Ordinary Business of Life*, by Art Carden

*The Anarchist Anabaptist: Essays on Radical
Christianity and Freedom*, by Cody Cook

TABLE OF CONTENTS

ACKNOWLEDGEMENTS

I am grateful for the support of many acquaintances, colleagues, friends and family members during the COVID-19 period and the process of writing this book. It is important to single out a few for their particular encouragement.

Two fellow ministers in my town were thoughtful conversation partners as I was developing this book. I was indebted to T. David Gordon's writings on worship, preaching, music, and media ecology long before we met in Grove City. Our conversations have ranged far and wide, and I continue to learn a great deal from him. Ethan Magness and Grace Anglican Church took me and my family under their wing in a particularly difficult season. During that year and since, I have benefited from conversations with Ethan about worship, ritual, technology, and liturgy. When I was considering whether the bits and pieces of writing could possibly make sense as a book, Ethan read them and said, "Definitely!" Ethan graciously gave permission for his painting, "Organic Glass," to appear on the cover of this book.

Brian and Shanna Tvenstrup have been long-time friends and faithful supporters of our overseas work. Brian took the time to comment on portions of this book, and also connected me with the Libertarian Christian Institute. I am grateful to the team at LCI, especially Norman Horn and Doug Stuart, for seeing the value in this project and shepherding it to publication. At LCI's request, Jacob Kim graciously read and commented on the

524

book—I thank him for his efforts and look forward to further conversations.

In this new global environment, one of the unexpected blessings of the online communication is the discovery of likeminded people all over the world. Two pastor-scholars provided feedback and support in various ways: David Wenkel, and Jamie Franklin. These men who have never met me in person nevertheless devoted many hours to reading, commenting, and advising me on publication strategy.

Special thanks are due to my good friends and former colleagues, A.J. and Michelle Howell. They endured much with us during COVID, and I will never forget their kindness and steadfastness. Michelle took the time to read this manuscript, lending the careful eye of a PhD scientist (biochemistry) as well as her courageous and sensitive spirit.

It should go without saying, but in a work such as this it is important to state emphatically that none of these people should be considered responsible for my opinions expressed in this book, or for errors of fact or reasoning that remain in this book. Indeed, some have significant disagreements with me! I speak only for myself, not for any organization with which I am associated.

I acknowledge with gratitude the ongoing research funding from the Department of Higher Education and Training (South Africa) and the library support that is afforded me as a research associate of the Faculty of Theology at Stellenbosch University (Western Cape). This research work is not the output of any specific grant, nor was it commissioned by any entity, including the University.

My family—Corrie, Daniel and Elizabeth—endured the COVID era with me. Only the four of us will ever fully understand or know what we went through. I thank them for their patience with me, and for always pulling me "out of myself" by asking me to play frisbee or Carcassonne. I am thankful to God that we were never separated—I cannot imagine how I would have survived without them. Over the years at many a gathering, they have protected me from greater social missteps: "Dad, you get *ten minutes* to talk about COVID stuff—then you're done!" Now that this book is published and I've said my piece, they can perhaps enjoy some peace.

My mother, Susan Soesbe, was with us in Lithuania at the beginning of COVID. I thank her for her endless love and tireless support of our family. She also lent her professional expertise as a published author and writing coach to the project. Mom: when you were trying to squeeze even a two-page essay out of your lazy fourteen-year-old homeschooled son—would you have ever believed that he'd grow up to write books?

In the Summer of 2020, having served informally for three years at the Klaipėdos Laisvųjų Krikščionių Bažnyčia (Klaipėda Free Christian Church), our local bilingual church in Lithuania, the pastor and church council approached me about serving as copastor, a tremendous honor. I had my doubts about serving as a Calvinist in a church with Anabaptist roots, but the spirit of collegiality and Christian love prevailed and prevented this from ever being a source of conflict. During the pandemic, each of us on the council had different opinions about how to handle personal health decisions and our life together as a church, but we navigated it together, by God's grace. In His mercy, none of our flock was lost during that time (to death or to COVID alienation)—a true gift of the Holy Spirit. These bonds of unity prepared us to respond to the February 2022 escalation of the Russia–Ukraine War, as we flexed our fellowship from bilingual to trilingual (Lithuanian, English and Russian), to support brothers and sisters emigrating from both countries. I dedicate this book to that congregation and to its leaders, my brothers and sisters in Christ:

May your unity in Christ and love for one another be evident to all, such that any person who enters your fellowship would say, "God is really among you!"

BENJAMIN D. GIFFONE
Grove City, Pennsylvania, USA
January 2025

CHAPTER 1 | Introducing the Problems

Why This Book, and Why Now?

As I write these words, it is now approaching five years since the start of the SARS-COV-2 pandemic. In January 2020, I was visiting Singapore for three weeks with my family: teaching a course at the seminary where my friend taught, spending time with my friend and his family, and enjoying a tropical holiday from the Northeastern European winter. When we were departing for Europe on January 15, 2020, preparations were well underway for Chinese New Year celebration, which is a huge event in Singapore. There were rumblings about a new flu-like virus that was spreading in different parts of the world, but no one had a sense of how serious it would be, and how our lives would be turned upside-down in just a few short months. Of much greater concern to us at the time was our return flight through the Middle East, in light of the US government's assassination of Iranian general Qasem Soleimani (January 3, 2020) and the downing of Ukraine International Airlines Flight 752 by the Iranian military (January 8, 2020). However, we made it safely back to our home in Lithuania (by a circuitous flight path), and began preparations to start the Spring semester of teaching.

In the middle of March, we went on Spring Break—and classes never resumed in-person that semester. Everything changed in March 2020, in what was truly a global event.

Five years later, COVID-19 is firmly in the past for most people, globally. I venture to say that most don't think about COVID much anymore: the lockdowns, the masks, the economic disruption, the deaths, the vaccines, the vaccine mandates, the travel restrictions—they are a thing of the past. Why do we need a book about it? And why do we need a book specifically about COVID-19 and the church—didn't the church simply experience COVID with the rest of society?

Even though the coronavirus that causes SARS-COV-2 is now endemic and much less concerning from a personal health standpoint (thankfully), the societal effects are continuing, and are only just beginning to be studied by economists, sociologists, psychologists, political scientists, medical scientists, and other researchers. We (academics, theologians, societal leaders and social critics) have merely scratched the surface. And, unlike other major human crises, COVID-19 was a truly global phenomenon. Previous "global epidemics" have actually been regional, or have moved in stages throughout the world over several years—whereas, because of the convenience of intercontinental air travel, COVID-19 spread globally within months, and the response was coordinated globally. Even the so-called World Wars did not affect all parts of the globe directly. Millions of people perished from the virus itself and from all the cascading consequences of the response. It does not seem hyperbolic to suggest that the COVID-19 crisis might in some sense be the worst thing that has ever happened.

It is therefore strange and unnerving to me that many Christians do not talk more about it today. This can be attributed to exhaustion, trauma, and the sense of collective experience (if we all went through it, what is there to talk about?). But, I argue, there is significant damage within the broader church that needs to be addressed, and healed insofar as it depends on the members and leaders of the global Christian church.

This book aims to be the start of a conversation about these hurts and divisions in the church. My thesis is that the underlying issues that made the COVID-19 pandemic so disruptive and divisive in churches—especially the North American churches (the places of which I have close personal knowledge)—preceded the pandemic, and continue even after the pandemic. I will demonstrate that the problems are deeply rooted in epistemology (ways of knowing), and the problems are exacerbated by the use of communication technology (in worship, in Christian community, and in social interactions), and brought to the surface suddenly by the COVID crisis.

An Interdisciplinary Public Theology

When I shared a draft of this book with my mother, Susan— an avid and thoughtful reader, but also an author in her own right, and a certified writing coach—she asked, "Is this a book of theology, a book about technology and society, or a book about COVID?"

After some reflection, my answer was simply: "Yes." A work of public theology, which uses the Bible and theological reflection to address challenges of the church and society, will inevitably be interdisciplinary, and will touch on several domains. My aim with this book is to convince the reader that epistemology, theology of worship, communication technology, and the COVID crisis are actually interrelated—and if you care about one, you should care about all of them.

The subtitle is "Technology, Worship, and Healing the Church After COVID." Most Christians recognize that we live in times of great division, and not simply because of the pandemic response and subsequent fallout. My premise, though, is that the church was *already* "A House Divided" prior to the pandemic, through uncritical adoption of technology into worship and the life of the church, and through uncritical adoption of scientistic ways of knowing. The church was divided within a "bowling alone" society that has seen decline in social capital and in-person civic engagement in recent decades.[1] Within congregations, individuals had further sorted themselves into affinity groups and social media echo chambers. Both "bowling alone" and online polarization may be attributed in part to the increasing technologization of communication. And even some church communities have been physically divided due to technology-enabled separate worship spaces or online worship, as we will explore in Chapters 6 and 7 of this book.

The metaleptic import of the phrase "a house divided" is the full assertion made by Jesus Christ: "A house divided against itself cannot stand" (Mark 3:25). These existing divisions were set up to be exacerbated during the sudden, sharp challenge of the COVID-19 pandemic. Anyone who cares about the unity of the church, its fidelity to the gospel of Christ, and the *missio Dei* should care about theology, technology, and the pandemic. Anyone who is paying attention should recognize that significant problems remain in the church, even after COVID-19 is past.

Exploring Epistemological Shifts

What links these issues (COVID, technology, worship) is a long-term shift in the epistemologies that prevail in society and in the church: how do individuals and societies arrive at true, meaningful, actionable knowledge? It might be useful to depict this shift in three figures below.

---

1. Robert D. Putnam, *Bowling Alone: The Collapse and Revival of American Community* (New York: Simon & Schuster, 2000).

Figure 1 depicts three sorts of knowledge, in a simple bar chart, presented directionally by the level of esteem or regard for each source of knowledge that currently prevails in Western modernity. These three sorts of knowledge are: "knowing through scripture," "knowing through ritual," and "knowing through empiricism" (or science, broadly understood). Scripture is revelation, whereas ritual and empiricism are experiential.

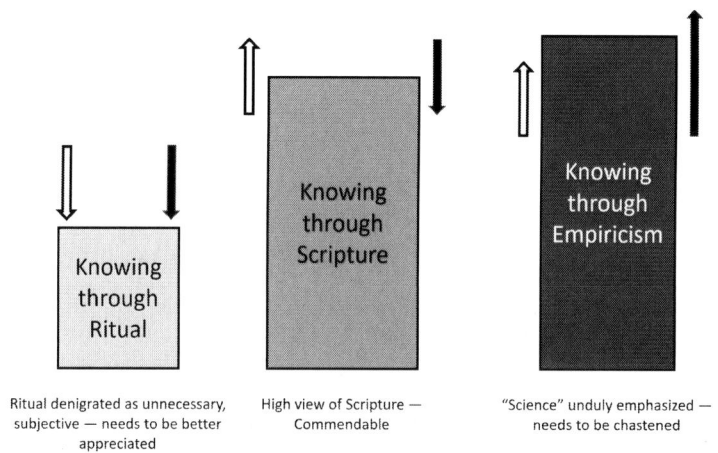

Figure 1: Valuing Ways of Knowing (Epistemological Foundations)

Christians have historically placed a high value on "knowing through scripture." The black arrow next to that bar represents the downward pressure of Western modernity after Christendom, and the upward white arrow represents the Christian apologetic witness commending the authority of biblical revelation over belief and practice.

Notice, however, that "knowing through ritual" has both white and black downward arrows over it. Religious ritual has been demoted by both Western modernity and Western evangelical Christians as a way of producing true, actionable knowledge.

Non-religious modernity views religious ritual only as subjective human experience. Christians may also regard ritual as unnecessary to the Christian life: if gospel proclamation, making/forming disciples, and worship are mainly about transfer of verbal/discursive content (spreading a message, teaching, singing, praying), then rituals can be dispensed with as long as the content is delivered.[2]

The third bar, "knowing through empiricism," represents the immense success of scientific method in the modern period. In this graphing, "knowing through empiricism" is more highly valued that "knowing through scripture." The long black arrow represents the upward pressure of scientistic modernity, which would further elevate empiricism as the primary means of knowing. The white arrow represents Western Christians who have enhanced appreciation for scientific method and all the knowledge that modernity has generated. The top of the white "empiricism" arrow remains lower than the top of the white "scripture" arrow, indicating that Western Christians would promote greater appreciation of both "knowing through empiricism" and "knowing through scripture," placing the highest value on the latter. The black arrows represent the pressure of modernity to attribute ever-increasing authority to empiricism.

The lesson of Figure 1 is that ritual ways of knowing are *undervalued* by both Christians and non-Christians in modernity, and that scientific ways of knowing are *overvalued*. This needs to be brought back into proper perspective. Figure 2 morphs this imagery from a bar chart into "towers" of knowledge, each with epistemological foundation and "bricks" representing insights in this domain.

---

2. This is an overly broad characterization that does not apply to all Christian groups in the West. As we will see in Part I, charismatic Christians tend to place a higher value on religious experience than do non-charismatics, and sacramental churches (such as the Roman Catholic Church or the Eastern Orthodox churches) value rituals as the means of conveying God's saving grace. Nevertheless, modernistic influences are found in even these branches of the Christian church.

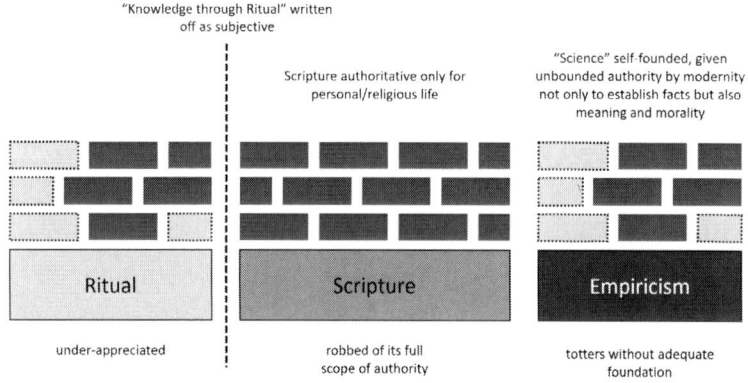

Figure 2: Domains of "Knowing," Improperly Founded, Unduly Segregated

In Figure 2, the solid dark bricks represent true insights, and the light bricks with dashed outline represent false propositions. Notice that on the foundation of "knowing through scripture," "bricks" of truth are built into a reliable tower. However, neither "knowing through ritual" and "knowing through empiricism" is an adequate foundation on its own. Thus, both true and false "bricks" can be incorporated into those towers, leaving each one weak and flimsy.

The dashed line between the "ritual" and "scripture" towers represents the suspicion of ritual on the part of many Western (non-charismatic and non-confessional) Protestants. On the other side, empiricism itself is not an adequate foundation to produce factual knowledge, much less meaning and morality. The middle tower, built on the foundation of scriptural knowledge, is solid but unduly narrow: scripture's authority applies only to matters of personal belief and ethics. Moreover, Christians who stay only in the "knowing through scripture" tower (narrowly understood) are unable to enjoy the solid bricks in both the "ritual" and "empiricism" towers.

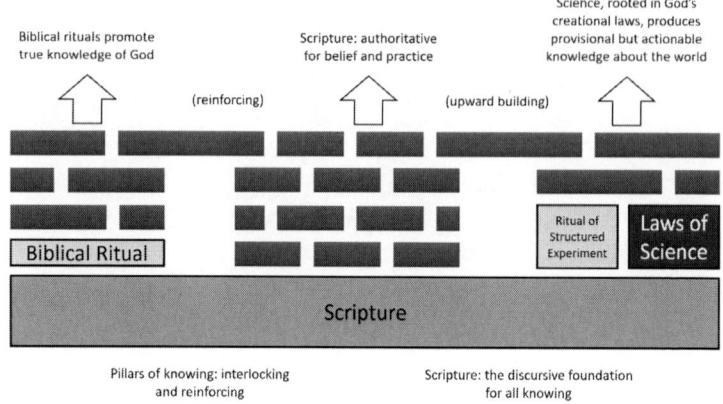

Figure 3: Ritual and Science Grounded in Biblical Truth

Figure 3 represents a proper grounding of both "knowing through ritual" and "knowing through empiricism" on the foundation of scripture, which is authoritative for all of life.

In Figure 3, the three towers are now integrated in foundation and interlocking in their upward structure. Ritual experience is no longer self-founding and purely subjective—rituals that are described *discursively* in the Bible, when *performed* with genuine faith, produce true knowledge of God (solid "bricks"). Similarly, the scientific enterprise is firmly founded in knowledge derived from scripture: the Creator God made the natural world with order that we describe (laws of science) and discover (through rituals of structured experiments).

In this book, I argue, contrary to scientistic modernity, that knowledge through ritual *can be genuine knowledge*, provided that the rituals are given by the God of truth ("biblical ritual"). The Western church has underemphasized the biblical and traditional ways of "knowing through ritual," including baptism, the Lord's Supper, worship gatherings, and in-person fellowship. At the same time, Western church leaders and Christian members of the elite classes have been too accepting of secular modernity's "ways of knowing"—*scientism* as a philosophy, rather than *science* as a method. Christian elites' anxieties about respectability unfortunately led to significant harms being done to individuals, to the church at large, and to society. These epistemologies need to be brought back into proper perspective, in order for individuals and communities to heal and reintegrate toward fruitfulness and flourishing.

These three epistemological pillars represent problems in the church that existed before the pandemic (and still exist), and explain how the reaction to the pandemic was what it was. In order to heal and to avoid it happening in the future, we have to adjust these epistemologies, bring them under the framework of the Word of God. Addressing the underlying issues that led to the damage of the COVID crisis will give the church resources to address other besetting problems and future challenges.[3]

Technology has been one catalyst that has revealed these epistemological shifts in Western society, particularly in the church. Prior to the pandemic, communication technology subtly and gradually contributed to the demotion of "knowing by ritual," non-discursive communication (which is more difficult to "technologize"). Simultaneously, the knowledge gains across all domains due to technologized communication has elevated the status of science and empiricism as a means of knowing—but not without costs to the message, the messengers, and the recipients.

---

3. The release of this book, by chance (or by divine providence), coincides with another that offers a biblical text as a resource for renewal in the Western church: Benjamin D. Giffone, *My Salvation Is Close At Hand: Isaiah 56–66 for the Church After Christendom* (Eugene, OR: Wipf & Stock, forthcoming).

Who Should Read This Book?

I am a Christian minister and a biblical scholar. In this book, I am speaking mainly to fellow Christians who regard the Bible as authoritative for belief and practice, and wish to give glory to God by promoting belief in Jesus in the world. However, I hope that thoughtful readers of any religious persuasion (or none) will find my arguments about technology, science and society to be compelling and interesting, even if they do not share all my assumptions and convictions. Anyone who is curious about how the Bible can be relevant to modern life beyond a very basic "be nice" morality that is the common caricature, will find that the Bible contains many texts that offer ancient wisdom for modern circumstances. Even though I have written this book as a "theologian" for other academics, I have endeavored to make significant ideas as unintimidating as possible.

I imagine that some readers will have taken up this book eagerly looking for someone to give voice to their concerns about the handling of the COVID crisis. Others will come to this book more wary or even initially hostile, perhaps having been given the book by a friend, relative or parishioner who feels passionate about the issues. To both the eager reader and the hostile reader: I encourage you not to leap to conclusions, and to carefully work through the arguments in Part I on worship, knowledge, and technology—resist the temptation to jump right to the COVID controversy in Parts II and III.

For a work that integrates public theology and media ecology (the study of structures of communication and their influence on communication), I hope that readers of this book will likewise be challenged through deep wrestling with biblical texts themselves. Too many works of public theology do not wrestle adequately with the Bible, beyond very broad categories of love for neighbor, justice, authority, etc. In this book, I have sought to ground public theology in the deep foundation of biblical texts (such as Leviticus, Romans and Ezekiel); my method is to let these texts speak for themselves, and then, upon careful reflection, construct models for interpreting present-day experience. The Bible is ancient, but some challenges are universal. My hope is that every reader of this book will be inspired to plumb the depths of the scriptures, regardless of whether they agree fully with my exegesis or application to current issues.

Why Should Anyone Care What I Say?

I have worn many vocational "hats," and have lived in and visited many places. Most centrally, I am an academic: a professor and researcher who studies and teaches the Bible, mainly the Old Testament. I have also served as a pastor, a chaplain, and a worship leader. I have academic interests, but I believe strongly in the importance of the church and strive to use my academic gifts to benefit the church and train church leaders.

I grew up in the United States, but have extensive global experience: PhD in South Africa, taught for six years in Eastern Europe, and lectured at seminaries in Ukraine, Singapore and India. I am blessed to be in regular contact with friends and former students and colleagues all over the world.

Unlike many pastors, theologians and philosophers, I have experience in "science-adjacent" fields. In a previous career (ten years), I worked for a pharmaceutical contract research organization (CRO) as a trial master file (TMF) specialist—so even though I do not have formal scientific training, I have some up-close understanding of the drug development and approval process. I also serve as a hospice chaplain, so I regularly enter healthcare settings and work with medical professionals in providing holistic care for elderly patients.

I experienced the COVID crisis and its aftermath while we were in Eastern Europe, moving back to the USA in 2022. I paid close attention to the evolution of COVID approaches and policies in various countries in Europe and states in the USA, as well as news from all over the world.

In my theological perspective, I am a confessionally Reformed (Calvinist) Christian. Even though the meaning of the term "evangelical" is shifting, broad and elusive—by most working definitions of the term, I would cheerfully use it to describe myself. I enjoy friendships and working relationships with Christians of all stripes, and am comfortable worshiping and ministering in both "high-church" and "low-church" settings. I am also a church musician, and have led music in various worship settings.

Having worked in both seminaries and universities, I value interdisciplinary research and teaching, and have published several works in collaboration with researchers in other fields, including economics and communication. My perspective is informed by an interest and extensive "lay" reading of economics, political economy, and media ecology.

Born in 1984, in my native culture I straddle the divide between "digital immigrant" and "digital native" generations. I have deep respect for the leadership and experience of older Christian leaders and scholars, and enjoy the passion and innovative spirit of the younger generation of Christian leaders—but find many points of misunderstanding between them, that I aspire to mediate (see especially Chapter 8).

Most importantly, I love the church of Jesus Christ. I very much want to see the church unified and thriving. Many of the problems in the church that I identify preceded COVID, and we won't dig ourselves out overnight—but we have to try. I believe that the gospel, when effectively proclaimed and lived by the church, offers the only hope for our fractured human society.

To anyone reading: I'm honored that you would take the time to consider what I have to say, and I hope that it can be beneficial.

An Overview of This Book

This is a book I never set out to write. My previous books for an academic audience were projects that were carefully planned, outlined, with a specific grand argument in mind. By contrast, this book poured out of me "at many times and in various ways" (Heb 1:1), out of passion, anger, sorrow, pastoral concern, puzzlement, and catharsis.

Part I explores the demotion of "knowing through ritual" amidst the technologizing of worship and discipleship. Part I began as an experiment: a series of posts on my website, written between October 2020 and the end of 2021, about worship, technology, science and the church. I have grouped these chapters under the Part I heading: "Technologizing of Worship Before and During After COVID: Epistemology, Eschatology, and Presence." These chapters offer arguments from scripture, sacramental theology, philosophy and epistemology—and informed by my experience in academic settings and a church, as well as my own study of the Old Testament and technology in worship prior to the COVID crisis.

Chapter 2 sets the tone for Part I by posing the question: is in-person worship an "essential service," and if so, how? In the Chapters 3 and 4, I argue that corporate worship is essential for human flourishing, because in embodied worship human beings *know* God experientially in ways that reinforce who we are in relation to God: his living, breathing images. Of the four "means of grace" (scripture, prayer/song, the sacraments, and the fellowship of the saints), two must be done in-person. To refrain from engaging in those two acts (sacraments, and fellowship) is to deprive ourselves and others of God's grace, and to open ourselves up to distortions of thought, feeling, belief and behavior.

Moreover, because human worship provides something essential that cannot be quantified by scientific measures, secular authorities do not have the categories to be able to judge the tradeoffs of physical risk versus spiritual reward. Thus, these tradeoffs should be left to individuals and communities. This is argued in Chapters 3–5.

Chapters 6–9 look at the thesis of "knowledge via worship" through the lens of media ecology, reflecting on what the introduction of digital communication technology has done to both enhance and impoverish church community and worship, touching upon the field of economics for the study of tradeoffs. Chapters 6 and 7 address the weakness of technologized worship according to biblical principles; Chapters 8 and 9 raise practical, pastoral concerns about how technology affects both worship and discipleship.

Part II began as an academic study of leadership in the book of Ezekiel, set within Persian-period reflections on leadership failures before the Babylonian exile. In a completely different vein, I had been collecting links and materials in the hopes of writing a piece on how the church needs to wrestle with mistakes during COVID in order to heal and move forward. In late 2023, I began writing both of these ideas separately, but began to see how the Ezekiel study could provide a model for church healing and restoration.

Part II ("A Plea for COVID Truth and Reconciliation in Christian Communities") is an appeal to Christian leaders and churches not to simply move past all of the mistakes that were made during the COVID era, but to address them for the sake of rightness, church unity, and prudence. If Part I addresses the demotion of "knowing by ritual," Part II addresses the undue elevation of "knowing by empiricism."

Chapter 10 begins Part II by responding to various calls for "amnesty" in the church and in society for mistakes made during COVID. I argue instead that reconciliation has to begin with a true accounting of what has transpired, and with repentance. I then offer four statements that provide focus and direction for Chapters 12 through 15: 1) churches erred in closing down corporate worship; 2) churches erred in segregating communities and treating certain people as "unclean"; 3) church leaders erred in using spiritual manipulation (binding consciences) to compel people to submit to COVID vaccines that they did not want; and, 4) church leaders were unwise/imprudent in abdicating spiritual responsibilities to secular authorities, who are not only not omniscient but are also in some cases openly hostile to Christian beliefs, and who engaged in censorship and manipulation. The first and fourth theses follow from the arguments made in Part I, but are further bolstered by evidence assembled in Chapter 14. The second and third theses are argued in Chapters 14 and 15.

Chapter 11 traces the theme of flawed leadership and accountability in the book of Ezekiel, drawing some lessons for Christian communities and concluding that God reinstates and rewards many failed leaders who genuinely repent.

Chapter 12 might be the most controversial chapter in this book. This chapter records and evaluates many assertions, mandates, and points of guidance from authorities which turned out to be factually incorrect. Chapter 13 reveals that, in order to protect their credibility, government authorities engaged in covert and open censorship efforts to suppress and discredit alternative points of view. Moreover, they improperly construed as "merely factual questions" many issues which are subjective and/or complex questions of tradeoffs and values.

Chapter 14 chronicles the consequences of errors, coercion and censorship for Christian communities. These mistakes by authorities led to a moralization of sickness, which was divisive, spiritually abusive, and devastating for individuals and communities.

Chapter 15 turns to the reasons why Christian leaders failed to recognize these errors sooner. I argue that evangelical elites (of which I immodestly consider myself to be part) suffer from a respectability anxiety that makes us eager to join elite causes to show other elites that we are not like the laity. This anxiety is particularly heightened around areas related to science, but has blinded evangelical elites (and evangelical members of elite circles in society and academia) to the fact that *scientism* is a new, false religion. Scientism is more difficult to recognize than other kinds of idolatry because, unlike literal statues of other gods, science practiced correctly is compatible with Christian belief.

What connects Parts I and II is the issue of epistemology (i.e., how we know things): scripture and the sacraments as ways of knowing God and His truth about the world, and thus how perceptive we should be with respect to other claims of truth and authority. This same issue of epistemology is the foundation for Part III, which offers a positive vision for the church and its leadership seeking to recover from the COVID crisis.

Chapter 16 offers biblical and scientific resources for Christian leaders to keep government and scientific authorities in proper perspective. Many Christian leaders outside of academia are unaware of the cracks in the "ivory tower" and the many academics who are publishing about the flaws in their own fields (and who often face great resistance for doing so). Concepts from political economy such as *regulatory capture* and *public choice* are introduced, to unveil the flawed incentives that co-opt the scientific process. From a Christian perspective, none of these governmental or scientific failures should be surprising. The response of Christian leaders should be to reaffirm biblical authority and an image-of-God based ethics that rejects coercion and censorship, and to recover a philosophy of science rooted in biblical epistemology.

Part III concludes with some practical next steps for Christian leaders and laity, and a hopeful epilogue that brings us back to the gospel as found in the book of Ezekiel.

On Sources, Citations and Authorities

It is prudent to make a statement about how sources and citations are used in this book. Readers will observe rather different kinds of writing, as well as different sorts of sources cited.

In the portions that are more theological and fit more within the realm of biblical scholarship, I have appealed to sources in a manner that is fitting with those disciplines: I link my own arguments with specific ideas of other scholars. All these works are listed in the Bibliography, in addition to the footnotes.

As a work of public theology commenting on current and recent events, I also cite numerous journalistic and online sources, which were assembled over a four-year period. This brings with it the well-known challenges. Online sources are fluid and can be changed after the fact. I am well aware that most readers of this book will not go look up all of the digital reporting, but undoubtedly there will be broken links by the time this book reaches publication. Of these kinds of sources, most are cited only in the footnotes—I have listed in the Bibliography only those kinds of sources that are more "permanent": books and scientific journal articles.

Readers will also notice that I have often appealed to what in previous eras would have been considered less-reputable and less-reliable online sources, including social media posts/threads, Substack pieces, advocacy organizations, and other independent online reporting. I have done this in service of a larger contention, especially in Chapters 12, 13 and 16: we are observing a massive epistemic revolution, as trust in official and corporate-media sources is diminishing.

Therefore, I wish for my readers to draw a "soft line" between the sources used in support of my theological, philosophical and pastoral points on the one side, and the reporting/commentary on public health and scientific matters on the other. Scientific knowledge is always evolving, and no doubt in ten years many of the "reporting"-type sources to which I appeal in this book will no longer be the definitive word on the issue (though I think the overall direction of my analysis will be vindicated). But the theological, philosophical and pastoral points will be evergreen as a contribution to public theology.

PART I

Technologizing of Worship Before and During COVID: Epistemology, Eschatology, and Presence

Beginning in March 2020, Christian communities around the globe wrestled with how to respond to the COVID-19 pandemic and the restrictions imposed to combat the spread. At the beginning, no one knew how severe the disease and the restrictions would turn out to be; few of us anticipated that the measures would last as long as they did.

Gradually, at very different paces all over the world, nations, regions, and church communities all over the world reverted to something approaching pre-pandemic "normal." In some places, such as my native United States, many churches went back to "normal" almost immediately. For other countries, COVID and restrictions were very much an ongoing reality for several years.

Though churches and societies have previously endured pandemics and other natural and human-caused disasters, one of the key differences has been the widespread availability of communication technology, which was further integrated into the life and practice of the church. Many churches had employed digital communication technology before the pandemic, but many more resorted to it during the pandemic and have remained "technologized" after the pandemic.

Technology, if adopted uncritically, can undermine the spiritual health of individuals and communities. Part I of this book offers a pastoral theological response to the pandemic, and a consideration of how pandemic restrictions and technology have restructured the life of the church (for better and for worse).

CHAPTER 2 | Is Church an "Essential Service"?

If a 70-year-old man receives a cancer diagnosis with a six-month prognosis, but could extend his life possibly two years by chemotherapy that would make his life extremely painful—is it moral for him to refuse treatment? What about a 50-year-old man, offered a ten-year extension of unpleasant life through such a harsh six-month medical treatment? How should the costs of medical treatment, and the burden on family, factor into his decision? Who is fit to decide such things?

In the midst of a situation in which a serious communicable disease is present in the population, should it be permissible to hold religious gatherings? What about funerals or weddings? What about Extreme Unction (also called the Sacrament of Anointing of the Sick, or colloquially, "last rites") in the case of someone dying from a disease that could be transmitted to the priest?

Is it moral to celebrate the Eucharist in the midst of a pandemic? How risky for the celebrant and the participants must it be, in order to be deemed too great a risk? How should the risk of transmitting the disease to others beyond the consenting participants be factored into the ethical calculation? How might it be acceptable to modify the structure of the celebration in order to reduce health risk? Who may decide these questions?

Is Corporate Worship a "Human Essential"?

In the early stages of the COVID-19 crisis, governments were faced with a rapidly-spreading disease, which was possibly transmitted presymptomatically: before the person spreading the disease had any symptoms. In a situation where human contact had the potential to impose tremendous externalities on others, restrictions on contact and movement were imposed. Most people accepted these temporary measures as necessary, particularly while little was known about its severity and its spread.

Completely forbidding human contact, gatherings, and economic activities, also imposed significant cost. Thus, many activities that were regarded "essential" were permitted, though often with restrictions. All agreed that medical and emergency workers should be considered as performing "essential" functions, as would those on whom food supplies depend. But the definitional question was rarely asked: essential to what? Is mere physical survival the "essence" of human endeavor? My pitiable upstairs neighbor, a professional tattoo artist who was put entirely out of work by the restrictions, laughed bitterly at his own plight, pointing out that tattoos are the least-essential personal service on earth for human flourishing—"even the brothels would re-open first," was his sarcastic claim.[1]

What about so-called "religious activities"—is corporate worship an "essential function," and how is it comparable to eating

---

1. In Switzerland, at least, my neighbor was correct: it was widely reported that legal Swiss brothels were permitted to reopen on June 6, 2020, roughly three months after the most restrictive measures were introduced, but before most churches were meeting. The "essentialness" of this work, by standards of modernity's conception of a human person, is implied by the COVID safety protocols proffered by a Swiss sex-workers' professional association: "[safety standards] cannot be monitored in this way but the same is true of private dealings between people and their doctors or therapists"—i.e., the sexual "service" provided by a sex worker is as essential as medical or psychological care. Tim Stickings, "Swiss Brothels CAN Reopen after Sex Workers List 'Safe' Positions That Won't Spread Coronavirus," *Mail Online*, 2020 May 28 <https://www.dailymail.co.uk/news/article-8365869/Swiss-brothels-reopen-June-6-safe-sex-positions.html>.

and medical care? The question itself demands a definition of the essence of human nature—a definition which, from a Christian point of view, must be grounded in the Word of God. Yet the temptation for the church in Europe (where I resided and ministered during the first two years of the COVID era) and North America (where I come from, and where I once again reside) is to accept not only modern science but modernity's scientized, impoverished definition of humanity. Among the Christian traditions, evangelical Protestantism, with its strong emphasis on the discursive, is susceptible in its own way to a bifurcation of body and soul, of private spirituality and action in the world—a bifurcation that undermines our human essence as possessing both material and immaterial aspects.

Total Technologizing of "Corporate" Worship

In March 2020, Lithuania went into a time of restrictions on movement, travel, and public gatherings—similar to restrictions in the rest of Europe and in the USA. Like most other churches, our small congregation of about fifty in Klaipėda decided to stream a "service" online, during our usual Sunday service time. The typical service elements included songs, scripture readings from the lectionary, a sermon, and a time of prayer. For the most part, the streaming was one-way participation on Facebook Live: we in our homes could see the leaders of elements of the service (singing, preaching, reading), but they could not see us. We could comment, including sharing prayer requests, and variously adding "Thanks be to God" and "the peace of Christ" at the appropriate moments in the service. Then some of us would meet on Zoom after the one-way streaming service for brief fellowship. I myself had the opportunity to preach in March, in translation, meeting at the church with only the music leader, the pastor (to interpret), and a camera.

This arrangement for a few weeks kept us connected in some sense: in our house we sat with our kids for the live "service" in such a way that we could sing along with the laptop, read the scriptures, hear the sermon, and chime in at the prayer time. But we certainly felt keenly the lack of embodied presence with the local body of Christ. As the first Sunday of April approached, a new question emerged on the church Facebook group: should we celebrate the Lord's Supper separately, simultaneously? At the last minute (i.e., Saturday morning) it was decided that we would try to do so. Each family was to acquire bread and grape juice or wine and to partake during the Facebook Live "service" at the appropriate time. At the time I was uneasy about this, but did not have a fully-formed conviction to offer to the discussion.

The Case for Embodied Worship and Knowledge through Ritual

Most sincere Christians attribute high importance to corporate worship. Worship is an end in itself—knowing and experiencing the Triune God—and an important means of discipleship, by which we become more conformed to Christ's image. By the standards of those outside the church, there will never be a justification for corporate worship that could supersede concerns for public safety, because society broadly does not have the categories to fully weigh the benefits of worship.

This book (especially Part I) aims to inspire Christian leaders with a fresh, winsome case for the importance of corporate worship, and how its benefits can be weighed against other concerns. I also draw attention to some practices of technological mediation that existed within evangelical churches before COVID-19, which have the potential to undermine the discipling effect of worship.

Back in 2019, I published an article focused on *technological mediation* of words and sacraments in worship, with examples from ancient Israel up to the nineteenth century, viewed through the analysis of *media ecology*.[2] This was of course before COVID-19 had upended our lives. In this digital era, evangelical scholars and church leaders are conducting more of our ministry and teaching mediated by technology than ever before.

In the following chapters, I offer some application of the arguments made in the 2019 essay, but also attempt to situate the dilemmas of the evangelical church during the pandemic within the broader conflict with modernity and secularity of our societies. I offer these main points:

1. Christians, while accepting modernity's insights into how the world works, must resist modernity's totalizing claims to define the essence of human existence in materialist terms;

2. Knowledge through ritual, including biblical corporate worship, is *real knowledge* that informs and transforms;

3. Modern communication technology has been permitted to restructure worshipping communities by replacing unity and presence with *mere simultaneity*, to the detriment of worship's discipling function—and this change was already well-underway before the COVID-19 pandemic;

4. The pandemic presents an opportunity to reform (and re-form) our worship according to God's Word. Certain essential aspects of worship cannot be facilitated (and are even undermined) by the use of mediating technology.

---

2. Benjamin Giffone, "Technologising of Word and Sacrament: Deuteronomy 14:24–26 and Intermediation in Worship," *EJT* 28.1 (2019): 66–77. The title is a reference to Walter S. Ong, *Orality and Literacy: The Technologizing of the Word. 30th Anniversary Edition: With Additional Chapters by John Hartley* (New York: Routledge, 2012 [1982]). The influence of Ong's ideas on my thinking will be apparent in this book.

The COVID crisis has forced many Christians (and people of other religions as well) to reconsider which beliefs and practices are essential for our faith. Even though belief is personal and individual, we structure our lives not simply as individuals, but as part of families and communities. Contexts and structures contribute to the meanings of words and actions.

Moments of technological innovation have the power to restructure meanings of words and acts, by severing and combining in ways previously impossible or untenable. As the church, we must draw on scripture, church history, and tradition to evaluate technologies, to recognize how they restructure our worship and our communal lives, to "lean into" some of those restructurings, and perhaps to resist when necessary.

I make two concessions/caveats at the outset. First, none of my arguments regarding technology are intended as a condemnation of those church leaders who in good conscience, up to and during the pandemic, attempted to use mediating technologies in the church while "keeping church, church," as a friend put it. I myself participated in mediated forms of worship that I would not wish to perpetuate. Parts II and III of this book do contain more criticism of some specific influential leaders, but in the spirit of reform, not condemnation.

Second, at times I will criticize the most extreme possibilities of certain practices taken to their logical conclusions—not always how they are in fact practiced by churches that are aware of the pitfalls/slippery-slopes and intentionally avoid them. The goal is to highlight these dangers at a time of rapid structural change in worship for many churches that may have incorporated practices without considering the downstream effects.

Measures adopted by local churches to temporarily enable communication apart from physical presence, if used uncritically or maintained beyond the crisis period, may unwittingly allow members partly to satiate desire for biblical teaching and song, but at the cost of abstracting the discursive means of grace out of the context of community, with deleterious effects particularly on the spiritual formation of younger believers.

While holding fast to our Christian convictions—and not rejecting the insights of modern science into God's world—we must recognize these underdeveloped areas in our traditions (particularly within evangelicalism), and take affirmative steps to ensure that our worship and community life takes account of the whole human person, body and soul.

CHAPTER 3 | Humanity, Danger, and "Knowing": Ancient and Modern Worldviews

How do we know what we are, as humans? How do we know what we know? On whom or what do we rely in order to determine what is safe and what is dangerous?

Definitions: "Modernity" and "Technologizing"

In this book I frequently resort to two terms, one of which is used in a rather broad sense, and the other with a more specific meaning.

By "modern" or "modernity," I mean broadly the worldview underlying contemporary life in Europe, in which God is no longer looked to in order to account for knowledge, coherence, and meaning in the world—having been displaced by human reason and will.[1] This worldview is associated with notions developed or advanced in the Enlightenment, including the autonomy of reason, secularity of the public sphere as contrasted with private religion/spirituality, and a general belief in the "progress" of human knowledge and ability. At the risk of eliding important differences between these notions, I am using "modernity" in this broadest sense as encompassing the ways that we think about reason, science, purpose, God, and transcendence that differ from

---

1. Colin Gunton, *The One, the Three and the Many: God, Creation and the Culture of Modernity* (Cambridge: Cambridge University Press, 1993), 28.

how someone in Medieval Europe would have thought. In this sense, "we are all moderns now"[2]—even Christians.

In my 2019 article,[3] I examined examples of "technology" that mediate within worship, and "technology/technologizing" were broadly understood as any human invention used in this way. In this book, *digital communication technology* and its rapid pace of change is the specific form of technology in view: the two-way transmission of words, sounds and images in real-time which can simulate human presence—in contrast to televised religious services or programs, for example, which have existed for decades but are a one-way transmission, non-interactive experience. The advent of instant messaging, social media, and multiway video-conferencing at a very low cost (the quality of video on a smartphone or a laptop being quite high) open up new possibilities for remote human interaction on a grand scale that were not possible twenty years ago and were barely feasible ten years ago. These technologies deserve special scrutiny due to their rapid adoption into everyday life, including the life of faith.

Purity, Danger, Ritual, and "Knowing"

Inevitably, one's experience of the COVID-19 pandemic in its initial phase was colored by one's vocation which was diverted, interrupted, or restructured by fears about the virus. My own experience of teaching, research, and ministry provides just one point of entry into these broader questions. It so happened that when Lithuania went into lockdown and our university switched

---

2. The expression in English, "We are all ___ now," was made famous in the realm of economics by Milton Friedman who acknowledged the dominance of an idea to such a degree that even those who wish to oppose it must adopt its key elements to some degree: "In one sense, we are all Keynesians now; in another, nobody is any longer a Keynesian." "Letter: Friedman & Keynes," *Time*, February 4, 1966 <https://content.time.com/time/subscriber/article/0,33009,898916-2,00.html>.

3. Benjamin Giffone, "Technologising of Word and Sacrament: Deuteronomy 14:24–26 and Intermediation in Worship," *EJT* 28.1 (2019): 66–77.

to online instruction, I was teaching an undergraduate elective on the Book of Romans, and completing an academic article on a topic related to the so-called Priestly literature of the Pentateuch.

The "Good News" of Rome: Tangible Salvation

As the Romans course turned toward the implications of the gospel for all of society, including the question of "gospel and empire," our readings stressed the artificiality of the modern distinction between "religion" and "politics." If we think of the Roman imperial cult and its claims to have provided "salvation," "peace," and "good news" of a "savior"[4]—Caesar—merely as means of political manipulation, we will fail to understand the tenuousness of daily existence for many within the ancient Roman empire, the influence of the empire on ritual practice, and also the direct competition of Christ's lordship to Caesar's.[5]

Imagine the following scene: A Roman legion shows up in a small town on the outskirts of the empire, claiming that they possess the power of a "son of god," favored by the gods, to protect this town from the chaotic forces that exist just on the other side of that mountain. The requirement is that the town offer sacrifices to Caesar alongside the gods of the local area (seen not as competitive, but as complementary forces); restructure their civic space to build a temple for Caesar and to celebrate his contribution to their peace in their monthly and annual rituals; to contribute taxes; and to support Rome if war were to break out. Though of course we know that in practice this imperial arrangement came

---

4. All of these terms were part of the rhetoric of the Roman imperial cult; see "General Introduction," in Richard A. Horsley, ed., *Paul and Empire: Religion and Power in Roman Imperial Society* (Harrisburg, PA: Trinity Press, International, 1997), 5–6. See also the detailed summary of the relevant literature provided by N.T. Wright, *Paul and the Faithfulness of God* (Minneapolis: Fortress, 2013), 279–347.

5. S. R. F. Price, "Rituals and Power," in Horsley, ed., *Paul and Empire*, 47–71; this chapter summarizes material from Price, *Rituals and Power: The Roman Imperial Cult in Asia Minor* (Cambridge: Cambridge University Press, 1984).

with a great many other downsides, this basic arrangement would have made sense to many ancients. Though in our modern scientific worldview we might distinguish between various sorts of "chaos threatening from over the mountain" and their distinct causes and remedies—demons, pestilence, barbarian raiders—the intimate connection between what we call the "physical" and the "spiritual" allowed ancients no such distinction.[6]

In Leviticus: Unknown Danger, Purity, and Trust in Israel's Sovereign God

Similarly, the Priestly worldview, with its understanding of sacred space, makes no clear delineation between moral and ritual purity. Protestant readers of the Pentateuch, accustomed to interpreting the Mosaic Law through Calvin's lens of moral, civil, and ceremonial aspects of the law, find that the purity laws themselves defy such discrete categorization. Some forms of ritual impurity have no correlation to "immorality" as we understand it;[7] for some immoral acts, no sacrifice is sufficient.[8] Sympathetic modern readers of the Priestly purity laws suggest rationales for

---

6. Price sees this tendency as "Christianizing" and individualizing ("Rituals and Power," 50–51), but one might also attribute this gap in understanding to the Enlightenment: "Scholars have often searched the imperial cult for evidence of real feelings or emotions towards the emperor. The problem with emotion as the criterion of the significance of rituals is not just that in practice we do not have the relevant evidence but that it is covertly Christianizing. That is to apply the standards of one religion to the ritual of another society without consideration of their relevance to indigenous standards" (Price, "Rituals and Power," 50).

7. For example, a woman being ritually impure during and immediately after menstruation (Lev 15:19–30) or childbirth (12:1–8); a married couple being ritually impure after sex (15:18); or corpse contamination (Num 19:11–13). Schnittjer rightly points out, "The concept 'unclean' does not mean physically dirty but ceremonially polluted or ritually contaminated—perhaps 'ritually challenged' in politically-correct terms." Gary E. Schnittjer, *The Torah Story: An Apprenticeship on the Pentateuch* (Grand Rapids: Zondervan, 2006), 329.

8. Note that covetousness (Exod 20:17) is a strictly internal sin—if it is acted upon, it becomes stealing or adultery. No reparation offering or restitution is required for covetousness (perhaps why Paul latches onto this strictly internal sin as his example in Rom 7:7–13). "Accidental sin" may be atoned for, but "high-handed sins," including murder and adultery (cf. Ps 51:16–17), may not be atoned for by sacrifice (Num 15:27–36).

individual laws based on science[9]—with limited success, because some prohibitions appear to be based on analogy or association.[10] But such explanations are beside the point. Regardless of underlying causes that we might offer, an ancient Israelite would have understood that unseen forces affect everyday life, and that maintaining right relationship with those forces is essential for survival. In the Priestly worldview, all of the sources of "life" (food, sunlight, rain, blood, reproductive fluids) ultimately belong to YHWH, not to other entities;[11] the chaotic forces in the world (disease, famine, wild beasts, the sea, goat-demons [Lev 17:7], lesser divine beings/gods) are subordinate to YHWH.[12] Thus, the fears of forces that threaten to overwhelm human existence are now concentrated: we need only fear YHWH.[13]

---

9. For example, the impurity contagion of surface afflictions (skin diseases, mildew in a house) mirroring microbial contagion (Lev 14); or the list of prohibited animals including predators (that themselves eat pests) and carrion-feeders (which could spread disease) (Lev 11); or postpartum ritual impairment as protection for mother and child from contagious disease (Lev 12).

10. See the groundbreaking work by Mary Douglas in this area; for example, the explanation of the difference between analogical thinking and rational-instrumental thinking in *Leviticus as Literature* (Oxford: Oxford University Press, 2000), 15–25.

11. "Some scholars have interpreted Leviticus by invoking a universal fear of blood, or the people of Israel's fear of corpse pollution. But the people are not afraid, quite the contrary; they are being taught about the world, and, the world being the way it is, they ought to be more afraid than they are. The work of the book is to establish an ontology. With formal symmetries and parallels Leviticus expounds the relation of life and death and the pivotal role of blood in giving access to God." Mary Douglas, "Atonement in Leviticus," *JSQ* 1.2 (1993/94): 109–130 [129].

12. For a compelling and thorough exposition of the Bible's conception of the divine council and lesser divine beings, see Michael S. Heiser, *The Unseen Realm: Recovering the Supernatural Worldview of the Bible* (Bellingham, WA: Lexham, 2015).

13. Taylor considers this a thread running through the Judeo-Christian tradition, which comes to prominence in moments of disenchantment. He writes of the reformist movements in the late middle ages, and of certain humanist and Reformation strands: "Revolting against all this ['white magic' of the medieval hierarchical church] meant facing a barrier of fear. But one of the potentialities of Christian faith was a reversal of the field of fear. The power of God will be victorious over all evil magic. So much is common to all variants of the faith. But this victory can be understood as that of white magic over dark magic. Or it can be understood as that of God's naked power over all magic. To draw on this power, you have to leap out of the field of magic altogether, and throw yourself on the power of God alone.

"This 'disenchanting' move is implicit in the tradition of Judaism, and later Christianity. Fundamental to both is a break with a world in which what they judge to be bad magic, the worship of pagan Gods and forces, is rampant. But this breach can take one of two forms; in a sense, it hovers between them….God's power conquers the pagan enchanted world. And this can proceed either through a good, God-willed enchantment; or else by annihilating all enchantment, and in the end emptying the world of it." Charles Taylor, *A Secular Age* (Cambridge, MA: Belknap Press of Harvard University Press, 2007), 73–74.

The temptation for those of us living in modernity is to offer a "god of the gaps" explanation for the widespread acceptance of the Roman cult and the ritual purity laws of the ancient Near East (including the Israelite laws)—the sort of account that Charles Taylor terms, "subtraction stories."[14] The common Israelite who adhered faithfully to the Priestly laws did not fully understand why the laws worked, but they trusted that the "experts" in ritual matters had been delegated special insight into the unseen realm.[15] The town on the edge of the Roman empire perhaps had a better understanding of the material benefit of the Roman garrison who protected them from barbarians, but also perhaps believed that devotion to the Roman idea and its gods was necessary to avert disaster. Whereas humans formerly explained calamity and danger in spiritual terms, so modernity's story goes, now we understand the material causes behind them—and so we can disregard the beliefs about the immaterial as mere superstition.

Modern Priests, Purity, and Danger

Lest we look back on pre-moderns with condescension, let us consider the narratives of public discourse in industrialized nations, including Europe, in the early stages of the COVID-19 pandemic. It was clear to the public that many people were getting sick and dying due to some previously unknown threat. Priests ("experts"), who were acknowledged as possessing special insight to perceive a menace that lay-people could not, began to instruct the public about forms of physical contact between people and surfaces that should be avoided, lest the force of death be spread unwittingly. They told us when and how to cover our

---

14. Taylor defines these stories, which he considers inadequate to explain secularity, as "stories of modernity in general, and secularity in particular, which explain them by human beings having lost, or sloughed off, or liberated themselves from certain earlier, confining horizons, or illusions, or limitations of knowledge." Taylor, *A Secular Age*, 22.

15. On misplaced trust in religious "experts," see Chapter 11, especially on Ezekiel 8–9.

faces; they taught us ritual washings for our hands, bodies, and cloth coverings.[16] Those possessing police power issued restrictions on places that we could go and certain kinds of contact that would be considered "unclean" and worthy of sanction with the threat of force, since even private actions between consenting actors posed a threat to the society.[17] Foreigners were looked upon

---

16. Some "priests" observed that a significant aspect of the benefits of cloth face-coverings was symbolic communication of the wearer's recognition of society-wide distress. In a widely-publicized *New England Journal of Medicine* essay, a group of physician-scientists suggested: "There may be additional benefits to broad masking policies that extend beyond their technical contribution to reducing pathogen transmission. Masks are visible reminders of an otherwise invisible yet widely prevalent pathogen and may remind people of the importance of social distancing and other infection-control measures. It is also clear that masks serve symbolic roles. Masks are not only tools, they are also talismans that may help increase health care workers' perceived sense of safety, well-being, and trust in their hospitals. Although such reactions may not be strictly logical, we are all subject to fear and anxiety, especially during times of crisis. One might argue that fear and anxiety are better countered with data and education than with a marginally beneficial mask, particularly in light of the worldwide mask shortage, but it is difficult to get clinicians to hear this message in the heat of the current crisis. Expanded masking protocols' greatest contribution may be to reduce the transmission of anxiety, over and above whatever role they may play in reducing transmission of Covid-19. The potential value of universal masking in giving health care workers the confidence to absorb and implement the more foundational infection-prevention practices described above may be its greatest contribution."

This is not an assertion that there is no practical benefit of cloth masks, though earlier in the article the authors write: "The extent of marginal benefit of universal masking over and above these foundational measures is debatable….And then the potential benefits of universal masking need to be balanced against the future risk of running out of masks and thereby exposing clinicians to the much greater risk of caring for symptomatic patients without a mask."

M. Klompas et al., "Perspective: Universal Masking in Hospitals in the Covid-19 Era," *New England Journal of Medicine* 382.63 (May 2020) <https://www.nejm.org/doi/full/10.1056/NEJMp2006372>.

17. In the face of the COVID-19 threat, some tight-knit communities, such as friendship groups or educational "pods," have had to agree amongst themselves about the level of contact they will each have with those outside the circle, to ensure a common acceptance of a certain level of risk. Cory Stieg, "Is it safe to have family or friends in your Covid-19 'bubble'? What you need to know," *CNBC*, 2020 June 27 <https://www.cnbc.com/2020/06/27/what-is-a-covid-19-bubble-and-how-to-do-it-safely.html>.

An analogy might be found in Taylor's description of the pre-modern "porous" conception of the self, as compared with the modern "bounded" self: because harmful forces can pass into the individual and thereby be admitted into the society: "Living in the enchanted, porous world of our ancestors was inherently living socially. It was not just that the spiritual forces which impinged on me often emanated from people around me; e.g., the spell cast by my enemy, or the protection afforded by a candle which has been blessed in the parish church. Much more fundamental, these forces often impinged on us as a society, and were defended against by us as a society" (Taylor, *A Secular Age*, 42).

Compare to the ancient Israelite cultus: given the sorts of regular, morally acceptable activities that could render an Israelite priest ritually impure and unfit to serve at the shrine (e.g., Lev 15:18), the priests probably discussed with their brothers and cousins (co-priests) their plans for intimate activities, to ensure that there was always a ritually-clean priest available to serve. Any hard boundary between "private" and "public" activities was artificial; private behavior affected the whole community.

with suspicion as potential conduits of this deadly force—some citizens called for forced expulsion of migrants.[18]

My aim at this juncture is not to criticize any of these decisions as unwise or unjust, but merely to highlight the worldviews behind these measures. Few of us have ever seen the microbes that cause diseases (and none of us has seen them without the aid of a microscope)—yet we trusted the "experts" who instructed us because we generally accept the scientific worldview of modernity. Our epistemology accepts that certain kinds of knowledge are generally possible, and so the hypotheses and remedies proposed by experts were plausible to the public.

In the next chapter, we study the significance of ritual in worship as a form of "knowing" about God that is essential to human being.

---

18. Nina Lakhani, "US Using Coronavirus Pandemic to Unlawfully Expel Asylum Seekers, Says UN," *The Guardian*, 2020 April 17 <https://www.theguardian.com/world/2020/apr/17/us-asylum-seekers-coronavirus-law-un>. Gaia Pianigiani and Emma Bubola, "As Coronavirus Reappears in Italy, Migrants Become a Target for Politicians," *New York Times*, 2020 August 28 <https://www.nytimes.com/2020/08/28/world/europe/coronavirus-italy-migrants.html>.

CHAPTER 4 | Science, Worship, and an "Epistemology of Love"

Thus far we have seen that a modern scientific worldview has difficulty accounting for the immaterial "essence" of human personhood, and therefore cannot meaningfully balance the risks of physical and spiritual harms. In this installment, we compare "scientific" ways of knowing (epistemology) with other means of knowing that are just as important for human life and purpose: knowing through love, and knowing through ritual. Knowing truth about God and ourselves by these means gives us purpose and hope.

Epistemology of Love

Materialism is not the only worldview that is capable of admitting the scientific method within its epistemology. The Christian worldview accepts that God the Creator has structured the world in ways that we can seek to understand through systematic inquiry. But the Christian worldview also accepts that other epistemological bases for knowledge are possible, and even necessary. This is not a case of "faith" filling in the gaps of knowledge, but rather: faith, hope, and love as a basis for true knowledge. Corporate worship is one means by which God allows us to know about Himself, ourselves, and the world. Discursive communication is only one dimension of this knowledge; God also makes Himself known to us "in the breaking of the bread" (cf. Luke 24:35) and through fellowship with one another.

N. T. Wright has offered this comparison. If one were to ask the question: (1) "Can a scientist believe in the resurrection?" which sort of epistemology is being invoked—the kind that is necessary to answer the question, (2) "Can a scientist believe that the sun will rise twice tomorrow?" or the kind that could inform the question, (3) "Can a scientist believe that her husband loves her?"[1] Questions 2 and 3 call for different modes of knowing, but both modes are based in past observation. Question 2 calls for a scientific epistemology, based in a belief that the natural world behaves in a regular way, such that we can extrapolate from past observation quite reliably to say that the sun will "rise" only once each day. A scientist *could* believe that the sun will rise twice tomorrow, but then she would be a bad scientist. To answer Question 3, the knower must also extrapolate from past experience of her husband telling her that he loves her, and also doing the sorts of things that loving husbands do for their wives. The husband's love has no doubt been imperfect; and, it is within the realm of possibility that her husband has been faking it all along, and may betray her tomorrow. But the longer their history together becomes, the more deeply that love is confirmed through word and deed, such that the scientist may say with genuine *knowledge* that her husband loves her.

Question 1 is actually two parts: can a scientist believe that Jesus's bodily resurrection is a historical event that actually occurred in the first century; and, can a scientist believe in a future resurrection. Wright is just one of several who in recent years have made the case through the lens of critical realism that Jesus's bodily resurrection is historically plausible, and even the

---

1. N.T. Wright, *Surprised By Hope: Rethinking Heaven, the Resurrection, and the Mission of the Church* (New York: HarperOne, 2008), 66.

best explanation for the historical evidence.[2] Wright goes further, however, in arguing persuasively an *epistemology of love* underlies the critical realism that leads us to true, actionable knowledge of the past[3]—including knowledge of the things that God has done in the world (most significantly, Jesus's bodily resurrection). In this epistemology, love is revealed through God's actions in the world—Wright specifically highlights creation, cosmic temple, Sabbath, and the image-bearing vocation—and love is necessary to truly know the world and the God who created it (and us). As we, with openness to God's love (an openness that God himself provides) learn about God's actions in the world, then Jesus's resurrection and our own resurrection as part of new creation become not merely plausible, but inevitable, to us. This "knowing through love" is not opposed to reason, but rather is "the larger framework within which both reason and subjectivity can play their appropriate roles."[4]

---

2. Wright, *The Resurrection of the Son of God* (Minneapolis: Fortress Press, 2003), *passim*. For his treatment of "critical realism," see *History and Eschatology: Jesus and the Promise of Natural Theology* (London: SPCK, 2019), 95–105.

3. "Part of the answer to all this is once more the epistemology of love. The point of love is that it is neither appraisal nor assimilation: neither detachment nor desire, neither positivist objectivity nor subjective projection. When I love I am delightedly engaged with that which is other than myself. Part of the delight is precisely in allowing it—or him, or her—to be the 'other', to be different. For the last two hundred years, as I suggested in the first chapter, Western epistemology has oscillated between the poles of objective and subjective, rationalism versus romanticism, logic and lust. The dream of scientism is for an objective certainty through which one can rule the world; genuine science explores and looks on in wonder and humility. The historian, recognising that all human knowledge is self-involving, learns to discipline the involved self so that the mind is open to different ways of thinking, to hitherto unsuspected motivations and controlling narrative worldviews. And, whether or not the historian calls it 'love', that exercise of sympathetic imagination is precisely the point at which the quest for *meaning* comes in, enabling us within the *task* of history to give an account of the past, which highlights real *events* in the knowable past and does so in such a way as to discern *the meaning or pattern of the events within the worldviews of the people concerned*" (Wright, *History and Eschatology*, 103, emphasis original).

4. Wright, *History and Eschatology*, 205–206.

Knowledge Through Ritual

Within this epistemic framework, biblically-revealed ritual becomes a means of receiving and establishing true, actionable
knowledge about God, ourselves, and our world. A scientist can
really know that her husband loves her because he and they engage in performative rituals together that confirm the words they
spoke in their wedding vows: they spend time together; they do
household chores together; they make love; they demonstrate loyalty to one another through times of adversity. God's relationship
to his people is likewise presented in scripture as a marriage (Hos
1–3; Ezek 16; Eph 5:25–33; Rev 19:9), and his love for his people is enacted in ritual as well as in word and in narrative. In the
Old Testament, rituals such as circumcision and the sharing of a
sacrificial meal (especially the *šelem*, "peace/well-being offering")
communicated God's continuing love and faithfulness to the human participant(s).[5] When we eat the bread and drink the cup
of the New Covenant, we *proclaim* in ritual, to ourselves and to
the world, the Bridegroom's death, until he comes again (1 Cor
11:26). As Wright evocatively concludes his discussion on this
relation of sacramental theology and new creation:

> The sacraments themselves, which like music form their
> own unique language to which all theology is mere pro-
> gramme-notes, might help us explore afresh the interface
> and the inferences between God and creation. They might
> also point us in fresh ways to what was accomplished in
> Jesus' cross and resurrection, through which, within a
> world already charged with God's grandeur, that same

---

5. See the excellent work of Dru Johnson, *Knowledge By Ritual: A Biblical Prolegomenon to Sacramental Theology*, JTISupp 13 (Winona Lake, IN: Eisenbrauns, 2016), especially 137–180.

Creator God has now dealt with the smudge, the smell and the bare soil.[6]

Just as mere performance of certain "scientific-looking" experimental procedures in a laboratory—donning a lab coat, pouring various liquids in and out of beakers—is not sufficient to produce real scientific knowledge, mere performance of biblical ritual is not sufficient to provide real knowledge of God and His world.[7] The discursive provides the framework for the ritual to produce real knowledge—previous scientific knowledge and the scientific paradigm undergirding the ritual of experimentation, and God's verbal revelation undergirding the rituals of baptism and the Lord's Supper for the church. God's Word tells us that he reveals himself to us in ritual, and thus the discursive and the performative are intertwined and interlocking.[8]

The gnostic bifurcation of the "natural" and the "spiritual" has convinced the secular West that only scientific epistemology can produce true knowledge, while other kinds of knowing are

---

6. Wright, *History and Eschatology*, 274.

7. On "the scientific use of ritual in order to know," see the insightful discussion by Johnson, *Knowledge By Ritual*, 120–133.

8. "Though there are indeed many 'psychological' or *non-physical* actions entailed in biblical worship, there are arguably many more *physical* acts of worship depicted in Scripture. These physical actions include baptizing, eating and drinking (taking proper meals as well as the Lord's Supper), fasting, removing one's shoes due to standing on holy ground, covering the head, uncovering the head, shaving the head, not shaving the head, tithing, calling upon God's name, praying, sacrificing, bowing, kneeling, prostrating, lifting of the hands, dancing, playing musical instruments, singing, reciting Scripture, teaching, preaching, and shouting 'Amen!' …Physical acts of worship are often rich in symbolism, in that they point to realities outside of the acts themselves. Just as the cultural mainstream is uncomfortable with the realm of the spiritual as anything other than a reflection of personal preferences, there is also a lack of sympathetic understanding of symbolism. Thus one hears that symbolic acts are 'merely' symbolic, not particularly meaningful in and of themselves. Participants invest acts with whatever meaning they may desire. Of course this impressionistic democratization of interpretation is completely contrary to the strongly referential purpose of symbolism. That is to say, the intent of symbolism is to convey meaning in a relatively obvious, self-explanatory, and often public manner, therefore symbolic acts by their nature are more purposeful carriers of meaning than non-symbolic acts." Scott N. Callaham, "Scripture and Worship," in *Dei Verbum: The Bible in Church and Society* (Singapore: The Ethos Institute for Public Christianity, 2020), 45–60 [54].

reduced to a second-order kind. It is this epistemology that precludes the possibility of bodily resurrection as a historical fact or a plausible future. Within this framework, "knowing by ritual" is impossible, unless it is the ritual of the scientific method.

Purpose—What Is the Chief End of Man?

In *The One, the Three, and the Many*, Colin Gunton argues that the culture of modernity has failed to account for the unity and diversity of human experience, resulting in fragmentation of consciousness, knowledge, and *telos* or self-understanding of humanity's purpose and direction.[9] Modernity's conception of time, the materiality of existence, and the imputation of meaning results in a paradox: modernity is ostensibly future-oriented, while unable to live in the present.[10] The difficulty is that modernity's "sceptical reception of tradition" results in a "culture attempt[ing] to live by the ideology of beginning all over again—the permanent exercise of creation out of nothing."[11]

In the context of the pandemic, we find that the crisis accentuated the problem of *telos* or "eschatology" that hangs over modernity's metanarrative (as it has displaced the biblical metanarrative of creation–fall–redemption–new creation): *to what end or purpose* are we taking drastic measures to preserve human life through lockdowns and vaccines, fostering economic growth,[12]

---

9. Colin Gunton, *The One, the Three and the Many: God, Creation and the Culture of Modernity* (Cambridge: Cambridge University Press, 1993).

10. Gunton, *The One, the Three, and the Many*, 90–91.

11. Gunton, *The One, the Three, and the Many*, 96.

12. "We economists are of course somewhat aware, or at least Frank Knight was, that we live in a 'milieu in which science, as such, is a religion.' Now, religion does not have to have a (pre)defined deity….Originally a religious idea of progress has become secularized into a technical belief that science can save us and that riches can not only make us happy (personal, individualistic heaven on earth), but also make society, as such, better off (general heaven on earth)." Tomáš Sedláček, *Economics of Good and Evil: The Quest for Economic Meaning from Gilgamesh to Wall Street* (Oxford: Oxford University Press, 2011), 235; quotation from Frank Knight, *Freedom and Reform: Essays in Economics and Social Philosophy* (New York: Harper & Brothers, 1947), 46. Notably this excerpt addressing climate change, expanding the possibilities of human life in outer space, or pursuing many other such projects? Modern secularity has offered a variety of *teloi*, none of which has led to vibrant human flourishing (and some of which have led to catastrophe).

The Christian metanarrative of the Triune God's relation to (and plan for) the created world can encompass and celebrate those desirable achievements of modernity. But we also must warn of the limits of modern scientism in terms of knowledge that is possible, and also in terms of the ends or aims of human existence that we cannot accept—or rather, that there are grander purposes of human existence than mere persistence of physical life.[13] In fact, there are individual and community aims and aspirations that might require us to undertake great risk to our physical lives. Just as the perfect image of the invisible God (Col 1:15) took upon himself great risk, even unto death (Phil 2:7–8)—so the image-bearing vocation[14] of those of us who are being conformed to Christ's image (Rom 8:29) entails risk of physical life in order to gain eternal life (Matt 16:24–27).

---

from Sedláček occurs within a subsection entitled, "The End of the Future and Modern Priests," by which he refers to fellow economists.

13. We will come back to this question of competing *teloi* in Chapter 15 of this book.

14. See Wright, *History and Eschatology*, especially 170–176; and J. Richard Middleton, *The Liberating Image: The Imago Dei in Genesis 1* (Grand Rapids, MI: Brazos Press, 2005), 43–90.

CHAPTER 5 | Christian Liberty and the Suspension of In-Person Worship

Some might object to any insistence on the essentiality of in-person worship, on the grounds that Christians are obliged to respect civil authorities (Rom 13:1–7), and should be willing to lay down our rights for the sake of others (1 Cor 8:9–13). Throughout the pandemic, some churches voluntarily stopped meeting for extended periods of time;[1] others defied civil authorities in order to stay open.[2]

If the government says we *may* not meet or *should* not meet, mustn't churches take that into account? Do congregations and their leaders have Christian freedom *not* to meet for worship? While these considerations should not be blithely dismissed, such biblical texts and principles cannot faithfully be deployed as justification for suspending in-person worship, in light of Hebrews 10:24–25: "And let us consider how to stir up one another to love

---

1. Kate Shellnutt, "More Pastors Agree With Andy Stanley: No Worship Services Until 2021," *Christianity Today*, July 15, 2020 <https://www.christianitytoday.com/2020/07/andy-stanley-north-point-church-reopening-2021/>.

2. Milton Quintanilla, "'Open Your Church': John MacArthur Urges Pastors to Reopen Churches despite COVID-19 Restrictions," *ChristianHeadlines.com* (opinion), October 12, 2020 <https://web.archive.org/web/20201027034943/https://www.christianheadlines.com/contributors/milton-quintanilla/open-your-church-john-macarthur-urges-pastors-to-reopen-churches-despite-covid-19-restrictions.html>; Esther O'Reilly, "What We've Learned From GraceLife Baptist Church," Patheos.com, April 17, 2021 <https://www.patheos.com/blogs/youngfogey/2021/04/what-weve-learned-from-gracelife-baptist-church/>; "Despite lockdown, Lithuanian churches to reopen for mass," LRT, 06 Jan 2021 <https://www.lrt.lt/en/news-in-english/19/1313722/despite-lockdown-lithuanian-churches-to-reopen-for-mass>.

and good works, *not neglecting to meet together*, as is the habit of some, but encouraging one another, and all the more as you see the Day drawing near" (emphasis added).

Within the long history of wrestling with Romans 13:1–7 (and related texts) and the relationship of the civil authority, with great diversity of opinion within the Christian family—there is unanimity in the tradition that civil disobedience is justified when civil authorities seek to prevent the proclamation of the gospel (e.g., Acts 4:19–20). To the extent that corporate worship is necessary for gospel proclamation and the formation of disciples (which we will consider in subsequent chapters), civil disobedience is justified.

Some Christian leaders argued that 1 Corinthians 8:9–13 should lead us to lay aside our rights for the good of the community:[9]

> But take care that this right of yours does not somehow become a stumbling block to the weak. For if anyone sees you who have knowledge eating in an idol's temple, will he not be encouraged, if his conscience is weak, to eat food offered to idols? And so by your knowledge this weak person is destroyed, the brother for whom Christ died. Thus, sinning against your brothers and wounding their conscience when it is weak, you sin against Christ. Therefore, if food makes my brother stumble, I will never eat meat, lest I make my brother stumble. (1 Corinthians 8:9–13)

Some understand this as support for the idea that Christians should not assert or exercise their rights to gather for worship, and pastors should not place a stumbling block in the way of their congregations by meeting against the orders or recommendations of government authorities.

This interpretation fails to account for the context of 1 Corinthians 8, where the end to which Paul exercises his Christian freedom (in refraining from eating idol-meat) is in fact embodied fellowship with fellow Christians. Laying down Christian rights to avoid stumbling others involves making necessary accommodations so that others feel safe and welcome coming to worship and enjoying table fellowship.

Thus, following 1 Corinthians 8 may entail significant restructuring of worship spaces and perhaps ritual acts for health and safety, in order that those who are more vulnerable may join the gathering with as low a risk as possible. We quickly learned several means of shielding the vulnerable, including meeting outdoors, physical distancing, and those who had symptoms choosing to stay home—and all this, before vaccines were even available in some parts of the world. Opening the church for worship and allowing individuals to weigh the gains of participation against their own personal risks actually respected the freedom of other believers; closing church indefinitely, for entire seasons, robbed them of knowing God's love in a way that is essential for human life.

Christians living under oppressive regimes have long understood that gathering for worship is essential for continuing in the Christian faith—after all, Christians in the book of Acts routinely violated government bans on worship and preaching the gospel (e.g., Acts 5:29). Though Christians in modern secular societies such as Europe and North America must guard against the "martyr complex," neither should they regard the secular state as an empathetic ally. Civil authorities in secular society, I have argued in the preceding chapters, do not possess the categories to fully reckon with the "essentialness" of worship—and will therefore never appropriately balance public health concerns with the need for corporate worship.

It is therefore the role of Christian leaders to advocate both for the safety of the vulnerable and for the rights of individuals to gather, mediating in good faith between the state and their communities.

Biblically, we must affirm that worship of the Triune God of the Bible is essential to human survival and flourishing. Human beings were created to give God glory, and we find ourselves living most fully into our image-bearing vocation when we worship. Worship is necessary for a kind of "knowing" that is essential to our human existence, and worship is the chief end of human existence (Westminster Larger Catechism 1). Without worship, we cannot know who we are or fully be who we ought to be.

Modern secular society does not have the categories to assess or embrace this truth claim, and therefore health authorities will never successfully balance this aspect of our human identity with other concerns (like economics or physical safety). In the worldview where "religious experience" is merely a construct that brings comfort, community and an ethical framework, worship cannot be an end in itself.

In the next few sections, we will turn our attention to "online church," its possibilities and its shortcomings, and the technological innovations that existed before the pandemic on which churches have come to rely quite heavily. Is "online church" acting as a placebo or spiritual "junk food" that prevents us from hungering for the real thing?

CHAPTER 6	How Did We Get Here? The Pre-COVID Road to "Online Church"

Merely demonstrating the inability of modernity to appropriately factor "worship of the Triune God" as a human need into its cost-benefit analysis leaves half of our task undone. Christian leaders and communities then must take the next step to ask: how much is physical presence necessary for worship that is truth-confirming and life-giving? When physical presence together has the potential to impose a health cost on some, how adequately can the biblically prescribed actions of worship be mediated by technology?

Christians have always known that gathering together for worship is not the entirety of the worshipful Christian life—singing, prayer, reading/recitation of scripture, and holy living are possible without gathering together with others. Yet even though Daniel provides us an example of private, daily prayer as part of diaspora Jewish piety (Dan 6:10), Jews also established synagogues for communal worship—and the early Christian church built upon this practice.

In-person gatherings for Christian worship have continued through some of Europe's most deadly epidemics—in eras when religious and political leaders were ignorant of the pathogenic causes and spread of disease. God's Word certainly calls us to humility, wisdom and prudence, places a high value on preserving human life, and reminds us "not to put the Lord our God to the test" (Matt 4:7; Deut 6:16).

Technology as Enabler?

The reaction among religious and political leaders to the COVID-19 crisis was striking, compared with the reactions to similar respiratory virus outbreaks in modern history. The 1918–1920 flu pandemic (so-called "Spanish flu") killed perhaps one to six percent of humanity (estimates range from 17 to 40 million deaths). The 2009–2010 so-called "swine flu" killed between 150,000 and 575,000 people globally. During these previous outbreaks, people still went to their jobs, attended religious services, and enjoyed sporting and entertainment events. Some became sick and died as a result.

Regardless of how we might assess the prudence of such actions (then and now), we must recognize the role of technologically-mediated communication in restructuring societal interactions, thereby changing the costs and benefits of avoiding in-person interaction. Most significantly, digital communication has reduced the cost of communicating information—through writing, and through oral and visual communication—essentially to zero. Much of the work of information-based or white-collar jobs can proceed in some form online, perhaps with some inconvenience. Because information jobs are the most productive as measured by financial income, tax bases in developed economies have not collapsed, allowing governments to still provide many truly essential services (hospitals, police, public utilities)—and in some cases, to provide support payments to working-class people whose jobs are lost or suspended.

The result is that restrictive measures undertaken and supported by those in the elite classes (government officials, university professors and researchers, journalists, many religious leaders) seemed less immediately burdensome to those making the decisions than to the majority of those subject to the restrictions. Technology has ameliorated the hardship for decision-makers, with the result that the restrictive measures likely persisted longer than they would have if a viral outbreak had occurred before the technology was available.

This is an issue of political economy which is important, and I return to it in Chapter 16. For now, it is sufficient to note that parallel developments occurred in the church, with positive and negative consequences. On the one hand, even before COVID, the easy digital spread of information has led to greater specialization within biblical and theological research, and also allowed local church leaders (and laity) access to information that they would not have had otherwise (or only had at great cost previously). For example, some material in this book was initially presented via Zoom to the faculty and students of a colleague's institution on another continent.[1] A former student of mine, hailing from one Eastern European country, living and ministering in another, was attending an American seminary online pre-COVID, and his studies continued uninterrupted.[2] Many academic conferences were moved online for the exchange of ideas, and some have continued online or in hybrid format.[3]

We all know that something is lost when conferences and courses move online: conversations before and after sessions, meetings, browsing for one book and finding a different one

---

1. On October 2, 2020, I spoke from Klaipėda, Lithuania to students and faculty gathered at Sattler College, Boston, MA, USA.

2. On the importance of continuing theological education amidst crisis, see Aaron Edwards, "The Perennial Urgency of Theological Education," *EJT* 30.1 (2021): 167–190 <https://doi.org/10.5117/EJT2021.1.009.EDWA>.

3. I myself presented a paper during the November–December 2020 online meeting of the Society of Biblical Literature, from the comfort of my basement, recovering from a recent COVID infection. I received helpful feedback, and that paper on Ezekiel 20 was later published in a journal. The relative success of the online meeting led SBL to replace their March regional meetings (North America) with a Global Virtual Meeting, beginning in 2023.

also—the question is how much is lost, and what are we willing to sacrifice for that additional benefit, in terms of risk and financial cost. When *mere exchange of information* is the goal of an interaction, mediating technology is beneficial. But if *more* than exchange of information is essential to the experience, then technology can actually *enable* a slide into less effective, less satisfying mediated practices.

The Means of Grace: Discursive and Non-Discursive

Even before the COVID-19 crisis, many Western evangelical churches had been slowly, unwittingly adopting—along with Western society—modernity's epistemology and teleology through (*inter alia*) our use of technology. The health crisis and the measures taken in response accelerated structural changes in churches that had already begun prior to the crisis. The logical end or extreme of some of these earlier changes was on full display as, for some of us, nearly our entire experience of the church was technologically mediated for a period of time. (A small number of homebound or exceedingly fearful people still engage church in this fashion, years later.)

One way of taking stock of gains and losses from introducing of technology, is the so-called "means of grace" as our categories: scripture, prayer (including liturgy and song, which constitute prayers prepared and sung), sacraments (or ordinances), and the fellowship of the saints.

Scripture, Prayer, Song: Digital, but Disposable

The first two means of grace, scripture and prayer, are fundamentally discursive (i.e., belonging to the realm of words instead of images or presences). Some of the earliest applications of electronic media in the 1980s and 1990s were the digitization and promulgation of the Bible—now, we have hundreds of versions of the Bible available at our fingertips. Beyond the biblical text itself, we find also an ocean of mediated discursive content, including text, audio and video; scripture, song, preaching and teaching.

This must be regarded as a mixed blessing. In our bilingual (later, trilingual) church in Lithuania, projecting the Bible readings on the screen meant that we could move back and forth between English and Lithuanian (and later, Russian to accommodate Ukrainian refugees) with ease. When there is a technological problem, however, there is no recourse—few are in the habit of bringing physical Bibles to church.

Outside of church, scripture is available to us all the time on our phones—but evidence suggests that we read it infrequently, in a distracted and decontextualized manner.[4] Beyond the pragmatics of frequency and depth of Bible reading, there is also an ephemerality communicated by the words of God that appear and evaporate on a screen—"the Word of our God stands forever," until it withers and fades on my Kindle Paperwhite.

Regarding prayer, liturgy and music: the use of screens, rather than prayer books or hymnals approved by an authority and costing something to print, permits the rapid incorporation of new songs into regular worship, which allows us to be more nimble—but also less deliberate and intentional about the songs that are sung corporately.[5]

Beyond the church service, the internet now allows us to access "the best" (by whatever criteria) preaching, teaching and music, which allows us to gain from the training, excellence and wisdom of others beyond our local body. But it can also lead to

---

4. See the research gathered by Jeffrey S. Siker, *Liquid Scripture: The Bible in a Digital World* (Minneapolis: Fortress, 2017), 57–96.

5. Jonathan Aigner, "11 Reasons to Keep Screens out of the Sanctuary," Patheos.com, 2016 July 18 <https://www.patheos.com/blogs/ponderanew/2016/07/18/reasons-not-to-put-screens-in-the-sanctuary/>.

dissatisfaction with the local church, whose pastor and musicians cannot measure up to the "big names" we can access online. Those online pastors and worship leaders have no knowledge of me, my family, our local church or community.[6]

Liturgy, Fellowship, Discipleship

One of the historic strengths of Protestantism, and evangelicalism within it, has been our emphasis on the discursive—at its heart, "evangelical" signifies a transformative personal encounter with a discursive message: the *evangel*, the gospel ("good news"). This is why Protestants have emphasized Bible translation and Bible access, and have regarded the sermon as the centerpiece of the worship service. But when our engagement with the gospel is merely discursive, then we risk neglecting or underplaying the performative/symbolic/substantive dimensions of our faith[fulness]. James K.A. Smith expresses this interrelation in terms of *liturgy*:

> Christian worship, we should recognize, is essentially a counterformation to those rival liturgies we are often immersed in, cultural practices that covertly capture our loves and longings, miscalibrating them, orienting us to rival versions of the good life. This is why worship is the heart of discipleship. We can't counter the power of cultural liturgies with didactic information poured into

6. Carmen Joy Imes speaks about this dimension: "When I signed on as a Christian, it was not a transaction designed primarily to secure my eternal destiny. Becoming a Christian means becoming part of God's family and changing how I live here and now. Spending week after week with these people, sharing this experience, eventually adds up to a network of caring relationships. It doesn't happen overnight (remember, it's a field, not a vending machine), but as we do life together, we lend support to each other on our faith journeys. Simply watching from home positions me as a solitary consumer rather than an active participant. While digital worship has been a gift to keep us connected during this strange season, it is not a sustainable way to cultivate the community of faith." "Church after COVID—Why Bother Going Back?" *Christianity Today* blog, 28 September 2020 <https://web.archive.org/web/20240714040339/https://www.christianitytoday.com/scot-mcknight/2020/september/church-after-covid-why-bother-going-back.html>.

our intellects. We can't recalibrate the heart from the top down, through merely informational measures. The orientation of the heart happens from the bottom up, through the formation of our habits of desire. Learning to love (God) takes practice.[7]

In relation to the third and fourth means of grace, the sacraments (or ordinances) and the fellowship of the saints, technological mediation was already leading to some troubling trends.

First, there is the phenomenon of the multi-site church, in which a live or recorded sermon performance is broadcast into an assembly, either in another part of the building (so that congregants can choose their musical style in the first half of the service) or in another location (other campuses). This is an extension of the "exposure to the best" phenomenon—we have a "pastor" who is really a *preaching specialist* on a screen, speaking to a group that s/he cannot see. Instead of extending to other campuses, why not plant a new self-constituting local congregation, with its own elders and pastors who preach sermons with their own flock in view? The multi-site model smacks of Smithian specialization that should not be a guiding principle in the church.

Second, technology that could have allowed us to organize and plan fellowship and discipleship has actually enabled our plans to always be in flux. This seems to be a general societal trend: firm commitments have been replaced by "maybe," or "I'll check in with you." But discipleship requires commitment, and "fear of missing out" undermines this necessary element.

Third, due to changes in our economic and social structures people move around more than in decades or centuries past, which makes it difficult to put down roots and stay invested in a church beyond weekly attendance. Do you know anyone,

---

7. James K. A. Smith, *You Are What You Love* (Grand Rapids: Brazos Press, 2016), 25.

besides a pastor's family, who moved house simply in order to join a particular church, or to be closer to a church? My brother and sister-in-law, in their mid-20s, admirably made important life decisions (where to live, pursue work, and raise their family) with church community as their primary consideration, but they are exceptional.

Conclusion

Even before the pandemic, "word" and "image" had been technologized with some extension of their reach—but with increasing fluidity, and at the cost of "presence," which cannot be replicated. Technology makes us *feel* as though we can replicate presence, but it rather *enables* us to persist in practices that do not really satisfy or edify.

In the next chapter, we consider how "online presence" for worship makes the mistake of substituting "mere simultaneity" for true unity and genuine presence. Unfortunately, "mere simultaneity" is the experience of many Christians in church, pre-pandemic—and I fear that this is true of evangelical, mainline, and liturgical churches.

| **CHAPTER 7** | Online "Church": United, or Merely Simultaneous? |

Worship and Community: "Unity and Presence" over "Mere Simultaneity"

My diagnosis of the problem in the pre-pandemic Western church is that mediating technology has allowed us to emphasize the discursive means of grace (scripture and prayer) while neglecting the performative (sacraments/ordinances, and fellowship/discipleship)—and that in practice the discursive means of grace cannot be fully effective in our lives apart from the others.

One aspect of this has been the substitution of *simultaneity* for *unity*. Even unmediated by technology, if the entirety of my pre-COVID worship experience has been simply passive and receptive (hearing and observing the preaching and the musicians[1]) while I am standing or sitting beside someone else in the assembly with whom I am barely acquainted—then there is little benefit to the incidental *simultaneity* of our passive reception of the information presented to us by the pastor or the worship leader. If this is all that church has been, then it is not surprising that people would feel little loss by introducing the mediating technology,

---

[1] Note that this danger is present in both high-church settings (Catholic or Orthodox services, in which the singing is performed by specialists not by the congregation) and low-church settings (when the band is too loud for congregants to hear their own voices, or the melodies are too stylized for the congregation to sing along with the band).

i.e., receiving preaching and music while at home—with or without a pandemic.

Can "Online Presence" Be Presence?

Few would argue that online presence is the same as physical presence—the question is really, what *kind* of presence can "online presence" be, and can such presence facilitate worship that does its intended work in the life of the believer?

In arguing for the inadequacy of "online presence," I wish to emphasize the *focusing, disciplinary* nature of physical presence. "Online presence" in one sense means that I am accessible and interruptible, wherever I have internet service—everywhere, and nowhere in particular. By contrast, an embodied person, a physical situation, or an object before me, makes a demand on my attention that cannot be easily disregarded. It is more difficult for me to be distracted from a physical book, than it is when reading a Kindle book on my smartphone with its notifications and endless alternatives that are only a tap away. If I am in church, I cannot pause the pastor's preaching voice as I can when watching the sermon on YouTube (where other videos offer themselves as distractions elsewhere on the screen). I cannot ignore the deacon in front of me asking me how I am *really* doing, in the way that I may ignore his Facebook message (or simply never get around to replying). When sitting in a hospital room with a suffering friend or hospice patient who cannot talk much but just needs me to be there, I am uncomfortably forced to learn how to serve that person with thought, word and deed in that moment, rather than sending my friend a brief "get well" message and then turning to the next task.

We are aware that we like to be captivated by an immersive experience, which is why we pay extra to go to a sporting event or a concert, even though watching a sporting event on TV or listening to a studio recording may offer better visual or sound quality—among other advantages, the in-person experience prevents us from changing the channel or interrupting the song in search of "a better one." Moreover, our attention is engaged by the other members of the audience present with us, as we are all attentive to the spectacular experience.

Focused experience *disciplines* my tendency to distraction—discipline which is necessary for *discipleship*.

The biblical metaphor of the faithful community as an irreducible *body* comprised of different parts possessing different gifts must be instructive (1 Cor 12:12–27; cf. Isa 1:6). The harmony of the parts is essential to the functioning of the whole (1 Cor 12:25–26). The gifts given to members of the body include both discursive (apostles, prophets, teachers, tongues) and performative (miracles, healings, service, administration) (1 Cor 12:28). The discursive gifts cannot be fully effective if extracted from (or abstracted out of) the embodied context of the church gathering, nor does the exercise of performative gifts have meaning apart from the discursive context of the gospel proclamation.[2]

It may be argued that "online presence" cannot *generate* fellowship within the body of Christ, but it can perhaps *maintain* or *facilitate* existing fellowship of an in-person community. This may be true for those already accustomed to the *disciplinary* (i.e., "disciple-making") practice of regular fellowship—maintaining a group chat to stay in touch with a circle of friends or Bible study group between meetings.

---

2. The "body of Christ" imagery in the New Testament is also related to the marriage metaphor of Christ and the church as his bride (Eph 5:21–32). Greg Wagenfuhr analogizes "online church" to two spouses maintaining relationship during an extended physical separation, but that physical reunion of the spouses (i.e., in the celebration of the Lord's Supper) should be the goal. "Online worship" should therefore be characterized by lament over exile, and longing for reunion. G. P. Wagenfuhr, "Is Communion via Live-Stream Communion?" ECO: A Covenant Order of Evangelical Presbyterians, Standing Theological Committee, March 19, 2020 <https://www.theology-eco.org/eco-theology-blog/2020/3/19/communion-in-exile>.

However, reliance on "online presence" may distract church leaders from modeling embodied fellowship practices for a younger generation of believers growing up with experiences of friendship that are highly "technologized" (this is the subject of Chapter 8).

Is Mere Simultaneity a Scriptural Value?

What might the Bible have to say about the value of individuals gathering *virtually*, simultaneously, for worship or other spiritual activity, using mediating technology? Of course, such technology is nowhere present or assumed in the Bible itself—we face a new phenomenon in human history, beginning perhaps with the telegraph in the nineteenth century, and continuing to include telephone, radio, television, and now interactive videoconferencing. In the Bible, whenever actions are conducted simultaneously in multiple locations, either the Spirit of God effects the simultaneity, or there is advance coordination (or both!). In every instance, physically separate but simultaneous acts have unity and embodied fellowship as the intended goal. Let's consider a few scriptural examples:

- Directly relevant to the issue of worship is the Sabbath, which is a universal simultaneous act. When we think about what we should be doing simultaneously with others while physically apart, Sabbath rest should be at the top of the list. Simultaneous rest and worship are built into the fabric of creation (Gen 2:2–3; Exod 20:11). In this simultaneous rest, all of creation actually follows God himself in resting, restoring, celebrating, and enjoying fellowship. It therefore makes little sense to extrapolate from the (ideally) universal simultaneity of Sabbath celebration, that we must layer on top of our family rest and local fellowship a *techno-logically mediated* connection to everyone, everywhere, who co-celebrates the Sabbath. The Creator God, present with his creation everywhere, effects our unity with him and so with one another.

- Building on the Sabbath principle, the Israelite ritual calendars coordinate several times of activities: things the priests to do at the central shrine; things for the common people to do in their hometowns (such as the Sabbath, or Passover meals); and pilgrimage feasts that bring the people to the shrine. As I highlighted in my 2019 article, God introduces technology (money) that somewhat restructures Israelite worship, in order to remove practical hindrances to Israelites gathering centrally for embodied worship (which involves Word, prayer, eating, and fellowship).[3] However, even the simultaneity of sacred time can be abrogated when exceptional circumstances require the delaying of communion through sacrificial meal; see the "delayed Passover" allowance in Num 9:1–14, expanded in 2 Chr 29–31.[4]

- Queen Esther coordinates an empire-wide fast among the Jews before she visits the king (Est 4:15–16). In Esther 8:8ff, instructions are given for the Jews to avenge themselves on the particular day that they were to have been annihilated. In this case, humanly-coordinated simultaneous

---

3. Benjamin Giffone, "Technologising of Word and Sacrament: Deuteronomy 14:24–26 and Intermediation in Worship," *EJT* 28.1 (2019): 70–71.

4. Benjamin D. Giffone, "Atonement, Sacred Space and Ritual Time: The Chronicler as Reader of Priestly Pentateuchal Narrative," in Louis Jonker and Jaeyoung Jeon, eds., *Chronicles and the Priestly Literature of the Hebrew Bible* (BZAW 528; Berlin: de Gruyter, 2021), 221–243; open access <https://doi.org/10.1515/9783110707014-010>. I also preached a sermon via Facebook Live during the COVID lockdown, based on insights from this article: "God Draws Near" <https://thinkhardthinkwell.com/2020/03/29/sermon-god-draws-near>.

action serves God's purposes, but still represents embodied action, presence, and unity (fasting, saving lives).

- In both the Old and New Testaments, we observe instances of divine healing accomplished "remotely," i.e., physically distant from the human mediator of divine power. Elisha tells the Aramean general, Naaman, to wash in the Jordan seven times in order to be healed—Naaman is initially offended by the prophet's lack of "presence" with him to effect the healing, but ultimately obeys and is healed "from afar" (2 Kgs 5:8–14). Jesus heals the Roman centurion's servant "remotely," taking as a sign of great faith the centurion's confidence that Jesus would be able to do this without a physical visit to the servant (Matt 8:5–13). These healings of people who are outside the visible people of God (Gentiles), along with other miracles performed through Jesus, the prophets and the apostles, communicate a message specifically about "distance": God's desire that those who are "far off" from him and his people would be "brought near" (Isa 57:19; Eph 2:13, 17).

- In Acts 12, the Holy Spirit responds to the fervent prayers of the church gathered together to pray for Peter while he is imprisoned (12:5). Their prayers were effective, even though it seems that they didn't fully believe they would be (12:11–17)! Here the simultaneous prayer and answer to prayer bring about physical reunion of the believers, and increase their faith.

- In Acts 10, the Holy Spirit addresses the Roman centurion, Cornelius, telling him to send messengers to summon Peter (10:1–8). The next day, "as they were on their way and approaching the city," it says, the Holy Spirit gives Peter a vision that prepares him to receive the messengers and to go to Cornelius. Simultaneity of action is Spirit-caused, and for the goal of physical meeting and unity of Jews and Gentiles in the one Spirit.

- Paul was trapped inside a Roman prison, and yet still discovered ways to resist and overcome the dehumanizing separation from those he loved. In Philippians 4:10–20, for example, he still had people within Rome who would visit him, and he wrote letters to the churches and received letters from them. He found ways to share fellowship with them, not just through letters, but through tangible things like in-person visits and sharing money.

- Finally, we have the example of Jesus, who could have accomplished a necessary task using technology (money) by hiring a slave to wash the disciples' feet at the Last Supper—but instead washed their feet himself, showing as their master how they should love one another (John 13:5–20).

Conclusion

In the Bible, every moment of "remote-but-simultaneous" action is effected by advance coordination or God's power, and *leads to a joyous in-person (re)union* of the human parties involved. From this handful of biblical examples, we might deduce that by contrast simultaneity effected by electronic technology is of limited value.

Media ecology teaches us that technology is rarely used simply to achieve previously-existing mediation slightly more efficiently—it affects the content and effectiveness of the communication. Once churches began live-streaming services on Sundays for the benefit of those who were homebound or immunocompromised, others who were capable of attending church in-person started to stay home and watch as well. With recording technology, even the simultaneity aspect can be lost: *I'll simply work (or hike) on Sunday, and watch or listen to the service on Monday evening…or whenever I get around to it.* Mere simultaneity for its own sake, apart from embodied presence and relational unity, is not a biblical value.

CHAPTER 8 | Online "Church": Are the Kids Really Fine?

In the previous chapter, I asserted:

> …Reliance on "online presence" may distract church leaders from modeling embodied fellowship practices for a younger generation of believers growing up with experiences of friendship that are highly "technologized."

In this chapter I develop this point further, because I find that this issue comes up repeatedly in my conversations with parents, fellow professors, and church leaders. Folks who fall into these categories are mostly older than I am (I was born in 1984). In my assessment, many of these older folks have not adequately reckoned with the differences that exist between their own experiences with digital technology in their adulthood, and the experiences of generations who have grown up with digital technology always being a part of their lives.

The older generations, having come of age in cultures of society, church and education that are formed by reading physical books and encountering peers and authority figures in physical space and time, are better equipped to transfer those educational, spiritual, and social habits into the digital realm and to cope with the shortcomings of digital media, than are younger generations. Put succinctly, we think the kids are fine, but they are not.[1]

Ten Years Makes a Difference

I am not a sociologist, or a scholar of media ecology or technology—so many of the insights I offer here are impressions and accounts of personal experience. I have been teaching at the university level since 2010, and thus have by now taught a half-generation of young people ages eighteen to twenty-two. Even before COVID pushed teaching online, I taught remotely for a university in 2016 and 2017. My ongoing graduate teaching for a South Asian seminary is mainly remote, with periodic visits. During my ten-year career in pharma, I was a senior member in a department that eventually spanned three continents (Northeast US, Poland, and India). I am not a tech expert, but I have some experience navigating these practicalities.

I grew up with personal computers in the home, for work and for play. As part of our homeschool education, Dad insisted that we learn typing. I also learned some simple programming in BASIC and C languages, which actually turned out to be of use in two of my eventual jobs. I got my first email address when I was eleven, and was active in AOL chat rooms and other fun online activities (mainly sports chat rooms) from that age onward. I built a Geocities page by editing the HTML code in Notepad. I was not naïve to digital technology, but my parents did limit the amount of time we spent in front of TV and computer screens.

However, all of this was via dial-up internet, which meant that the experience was limited to certain times of day (because it tied

---

1. A growing body of academic literature on the effects of social media on preteens and teenagers is confirming this fact. A good starting point is Jonathan Haidt, *The Anxious Generation: How the Great Rewiring of Childhood Is Causing an Epidemic of Mental Illness* (New York: Penguin Press, 2024); and Haidt's Substack, "After Babel," which has several contributors (<https://www.afterbabel.com>).

up the phone line) and also to an essentially text-only experience. We did not get high-speed (DSL, still glacial by today's standards) until 2003, late in my senior year of high school. At university from 2003–2006, there was DSL (or something comparable) in the residence halls and apartments, and the internet was starting to become more interesting with images loading faster (though sometimes still line-by-line). Smart phones, social media and streaming video did not exist. I emailed friends and chatted in real time on AIM, but mainly my social life consisted of calls and hanging out in person. I got my first cell phone when I went to college, but it could only make calls and send text messages.

Throughout my primary, secondary, and university education, the main form of content delivery was physical books, including great works of history and literature, textbooks, workbooks, and reference books like encyclopedias and commentaries. My parents did explain things to us orally ("lecture" and discussion), and we did attend group classes with other homeschoolers. My university experience was a typical mix of reading, lectures, discussion, and writing. I used the card catalog to find books in the library. Online resources were still not that helpful; we mainly used internet to email professors and (eventually) to search the library catalog.

By comparison, my brother, who is ten years younger than I, grew up with a very different experience of digital technology. He was eight years old when we got DSL in the home, and got an iPod Touch with wifi internet and some streaming video capability when he was almost twelve. By then, Facebook was starting to enjoy widespread use. He had a texting app and messaged his friends all the time—whereas when I was in middle and high school, if I wanted to phone a friend, I could only call his/her home landline (only at certain times) to speak with him/her. When I was a teen, I had to work, save up, and purchase CDs in order to have new music; by the time my brother was eighteen, all music and movies were basically free on YouTube or streaming sites (of varying costs and degrees of legality).

Sexualization

Older readers can probably think of myriad ways that their own educational, social and spiritual formation might have been affected by having unlimited and constant access to information, audio, video, and friends during the ages of 12 to 22. To point out one that is crucial for young men especially (but also for young women), I can vaguely remember the first time I saw nude images on the internet, my senior year of high school after we got DSL. I had previously seen images I found titillating only in catalogs or circulars (clothing ads), and on magazine covers in the store. Even the nude images I saw (no videos at that time) would be considered hopelessly tame compared to what is easily available on the internet today.

And so, I went off to university with a problem of secretly looking lustfully at inappropriate images on the internet. Thankfully, there was a culture in the dorm of other Christian young men who were similarly struggling, and who would support one another and keep each other accountable. Many of us kept our computers out in the common room so that we did not have private access. I cannot claim that I have never since then violated Jesus's command in Matthew 5:27–30. But I am grateful that I at least had the tools from my spiritual formation in church community up to that point, and the community of believers around me in college, to recognize and to fight the sin of lust—and I'm grateful that my first real struggle with this sin was not until I was seventeen.

Fast forward to the present: we have abundant research showing that children as young as seven are exposed to pornography, the majority by age thirteen,[2] and that this has consequences for

---

2. "What's the Average Age of a Child's First Exposure to Porn?" *FightTheNewDrug.org*, n.d. <https://fightthenewdrug.org/real-average-age-of-first-exposure>.

their sexuality[3] (and their spiritual formation). I cannot imagine how my experience with temptation would have been different had I had internet access when I was eight or twelve. Suffice to say: absent parental supervision, boys and girls today are being trained to view bodies (mostly girls' and women's bodies) as objects, public property for consumption, evaluation, approval, ridicule, and private enjoyment. This is clearly linked not only to the availability of pictures and videos, but to social media, which allows real-time sharing of one's own images and videos for evaluation by peers (and anyone with whom they share it).

Greater availability of sexualized images, combined with technologized (i.e., skewed) sense of friendship and community, is a toxic mix for children and teens. It is an understatement to assert that parents should be aware and attentive to these dangers, and strongly consider taking those tablets and smart phones away from their kids.

More Benign Stimulation

The development of sexual awareness and its relation to personal holiness is just one minefield that has become even more complicated in the age of digital technology. Even when we consider more benign digital content than pornography and sexting, it is clear that consumption of videos and images, and of words via screens rather than printed text, is affecting attention spans—particularly, those whose media consumption habits were formed in the digital age.

Even though Americans (though I assume this applies in other countries as well) have watched a lot of television for a long time, at least those who went to school before the 2000s were forced to

---

3. Kate Julian, "The Sex Recession: Why Are Young People Having So Little Sex?" *The Atlantic*, Dec 2018 <https://www.theatlantic.com/magazine/archive/2018/12/the-sex-recession/573949/>.

read books in school, so that they have at least the mental muscle memory of reading texts, in those formative stages of brain development. Nowadays, much content that could be communicated in digital text is presented in video, which is a qualitatively different medium, and immensely stimulating–perhaps too stimulating to think critically about. And the visual content today is just objectively more pleasant and stimulating to watch than the TV and movies of twenty-five years ago.

Moreover, reading digital text is simply different from reading text on a page. Again, this is not my area of expertise, but there is a great deal of research and reporting on this, and I have observed it in my own reading experience, and with students. Certainly since I started teaching in 2010, I think that the ability of American and European nineteen-year-olds to read and critically assess texts has declined.

I observe an even sharper decline in the students' comprehension when they read articles digitally. A few years ago, I began providing them with spiral-bound printed packets of the readings (articles and chapters) for the semester (still much cheaper than buying books), and that helped tremendously, especially if I required them to bring the packets to class and read aloud from them for the purpose of discussion. I also typically forbade the use of electronics in my classes for note-taking or reading (for undergrads), so the physical packets and Bibles (required) made discussion possible. Several students remarked on how much easier it is to read the texts without distraction, and they liked being able to mark up the articles on printed packets.

By comparison, in the lockdown-plagued academic years, I was unable to provide printed packets and to forbid electronics, when instruction was via videoconferencing and the students were scattered all over the world. The engagement with the texts and in the classroom definitely suffered—most students even recognized this for themselves.

Digital Natives in the Ecosystem of "Online Church"

What does this all mean for church? Coming back around to the generational gap: at the risk of solipsism, I really do believe that I and those who graduated from high school in the early 2000s (some might call us older millennials) straddle this digital divide. When it comes to online engagement with "church" content and activities, those who are older than us still conceive of online engagement essentially in terms of watching [a sermon], listening [to a song], and reading [biblical text] as if these were in-person experiences, merely replicated digitally—somewhat more conveniently, a little less satisfying, but still effective.

Even we who are "digital immigrants" (those who reached adulthood *before* the digital information explosion) are being changed by visual and social media, and not for the better. Our attention spans, our ability to read, and our psychological health are detrimentally affected. But we digital immigrants at least have a sense of what we used to be able to do, and some ability to push back a bit in reshaping our habits. Digital natives (those who grew up with digital technology) do not even have a sense of what is possible for them apart from digital engagement/reading. Similarly, it is *more attainable* for digital immigrants to engage an online sermon *not* as we would engage a typical online video (not ideal) but as we would engage an in-person sermon (the aim), because digital immigrants have years and years of experience having to focus while listening to live speakers (teachers, professors, pastors). It is much more difficult for digital natives to make this distinction between different kinds of online video, to engage a sermon in the same way they would engage an in-person lecture or music performance. The medium itself and the myriad distractions that they are used to being offered alongside this video (as I mentioned in Chapter 7) make the experience of "online sermon" indistinguishable from the experience of other videos, despite the best efforts of viewer to focus and engage.

Nearly all churches are broadcasting services online. I have spoken with many pastors and lay leaders about this new phenomenon, and asked their sense of the pluses and minuses, as well as their own personal engagement with streaming. Invariably, those who express some sort of excitement about the new technologized broadcast bringing people into the church (or connecting with younger people) are *older* than I am (i.e., born before 1984). Those who are younger, or older friends who are speaking about their own kids' engagement with online services, are much more pessimistic about this, and I think they are correct to be pessimistic.

It is possible that some people will search for truth and encouragement in times of crisis, find online church engagement, and eventually end up coming to church. We should pray that this will happen. But I doubt it will be nearly as many as those who get bored with online "church" and just stop watching altogether—without ever coming back. Emerging research suggests the latter (see Chapter 14).

The reason is simple: there is an ocean of better content elsewhere on the internet (see Chapter 6). There is always a better preacher, a better choir, a better worship band out there. Why watch a poor livestream from the back of the sanctuary, or even a polished recorded presentation, when one can curate one's own preferred combination of high-quality (however defined) liturgy, music and teaching? The mediocre livestream may be acceptable for a time, provided there are existing relationships and commitment that can be maintained through a period of crisis. But building church relationships and commitment in this way is impossible.

CHAPTER 9 | Online "Church": Performativity, Privacy, Scrutiny

I have expressed many concerns about the continuation of "online church," that is, online streaming and recording of church services to be consumed by members of the congregation and the general public. In the last chapter, we discussed the influence of online technology and engagement on younger audiences. This chapter addresses two structural issues raised by "online church": how the online format affects the content of the service and the message, and the practical concerns about opening the local congregation and its members to unwelcome attention.

What Can "Online Church" Mean?

Before I raise my additional concerns, several distinctions are necessary. The idea of "online church" usually centers around giving people at home something spiritually edifying to do on Sunday (or later!), and to remain connected to the local church when they choose not to gather with others, or when gathering is prevented for some reason. But forming an online service entails choosing from a variety of formats:

- First, what precisely is being transmitted online? Some churches present only the sermon, which is the most difficult element of the service for the lay person to "replicate" at home. Other churches provide recording/streaming of all elements of the service, including songs, scripture readings and prayers. Sometimes, this may also include the sharing of personal prayer requests, or otherwise engaging with people from the congregation other than those who have chosen to step up, in front of the camera.

In "the old days," churches might provide recordings of sermons on tape, CD, or audio download. The church I worked for in Pennsylvania would have a sermon from a previous week broadcast on AM radio on Sunday mornings. Nowadays, when time and storage space is not an issue, churches have been including songs, readings, and other service elements in the broadcast as well. Multi-site churches, as I discussed in Chapter 6, made recording and broadcast technology central to their normal services even before COVID.

• Second, churches can choose to present video of services, or audio only. This difference certainly matters for how digital presentation is generated and received. Some preachers rely on presentations and other images in their sermons; others are purely discursive (I tend to be the latter). Some churches might also have theological objections to the use of (moving) images in worship. Others might find it distracting for viewers.

• Third, there are choices as to when the service is recorded and when it is presented. A service can be recorded in advance (perhaps in a studio), and designed specifically for online presentation. A service can be streamed live online, but not recorded/preserved for later consumption (stream only). A live-streamed service can be recorded for later, as presented. Finally, a live recording could be presented later (not simultaneous), after editing.

In the midst of the COVID-19 pandemic (and to this day), some churches produced their service elements fully in advance, often in a studio-like setting, with the pastor and worship leaders sometimes looking directly into the camera. Other churches have simply transmitted from the live service onto the web. Studios and video editing pose not insignificant costs for churches who choose to go this route.

- Finally, there is the question of who may access the service online: is it only for members and those with a previous connection to the church who know to look for it (e.g., unlisted YouTube video, linked from church's website)? Or, is it on a public channel where it's relatively easy to find and share?

This last issue is probably one of the most important for what I will raise below. Chapters 6 and 7 focused extensively on the negative effect of online church service that permits those who *could* attend church in person to feel like they are getting something beneficial, but actually prevents them from receiving the full benefit of gathering in community for worship. I still feel that this is a grave concern. But in this chapter, I take as a given that some people really want to engage and remain connected to church, but cannot always come, for some compelling reason.

Performativity: Preaching to the Crowd, or to the Camera?

My first additional concern is that the very fact of having a service (or some element) recorded or streamed could lead to the music or sermon becoming more performative than it otherwise would be. Now, there is always a dramatic dimension to music and preaching–in worship, we should be reenacting God's drama of redemption. But just as watching a live performance of a play is different from that play adapted for the screen, so music and preaching may be affected when the camera is present.

Within *Christianity Today*'s podcast series, "The Rise and Fall of Mars Hill,"[1] there is a moment in Mars Hill's development that stood out to the producer/writer as quite significant: a dramatic high point of a sermon in which Driscoll yelled, "How dare you! Who do you think you are?!" at a specific segment of the congregation, apparently with spontaneous pastoral/prophetic zeal. This moment was quickly excerpted and went viral. But it later became clear that this was planned, and occurred in all of Driscoll's "performances" of this sermon in the various services. The presence of the camera seems to have prompted him to plan this particular dramatic turn in his sermon. It is hard not to see this as manipulative (curious readers may find the clip online and judge for themselves).

Most churches do not have the same online reach that Mars Hill did. But the question of: for whom are we producing this service, is still relevant. When it comes to pre-recording and online streaming, small local churches face a choice: either do the online stream without any features for the sake of online viewers (just a camera in the back)—or, orient the service preparation and rehearsal toward online production, which can detract from the in-person service. In the latter situation, the congregants who are physically present start to wonder whether the service is "for them" or for those online—when it should be a service *with* them: they are full participants in the service.

---

1. Mike Cosper, "The Rise and Fall of Mars Hill," *Christianity Today* <https://www.christianity today.com/podcasts/the-rise-and-fall-of-mars-hill/>

Privacy: The Church as Safe Haven

A second issue is the sharing of personal information when a camera is present. Here the concerns are performativity, and privacy. Younger people, including younger pastors and worship leaders, are simply more accustomed to sharing more of our lives online, publicly. We are more comfortable talking about (socially-approved) personal struggles, including mental health issues. But this can lead to an unhealthy performativity for those in front of the camera (pastor and worship leaders), and those who might be present and wish to share prayer requests in the service.

Regarding privacy, some people are less comfortable sharing when they know it can go out on the internet. I myself have experienced this on a few occasions. I mostly preach in contexts where only my wife and kids are present—not extended family. I have occasionally self-censored or spoken intentionally vaguely about extended family members—partly to avoid being distracting in a sermon, but partly because I do not want a family member (or friend) who is not present to hear me talking about him or her identifiably on the internet. It is unlikely that they would seek out my sermons and listen, but I prefer not to take that chance.

Prayer requests can be even more sensitive when it comes to privacy. Some people are shy; they might feel comfortable sharing intimate life concerns in a local church setting, but do not want such prayer requests mentioned on the web. Some are from countries, or in sensitive family and job situations, such that they could face harm (persecution, domestic abuse) if the wrong people found out that they attend a Christian church, or this church in particular. People should feel safe and protected in the church, and not be concerned that their faces or problems could be broadcast.

Scrutiny: Woke Corporations are Watching

> "Rabbi, is there a blessing for the tsar?" "Of course!
> 'May G-d bless and keep the tsar...far away from us!'"
> —Sheldon Harnick, *Fiddler on the Roof*

A third concern is that "online church" can expose local churches to scrutiny that could result in legal or censorship action. There is the copyright issue when it comes to recording songs—this is beyond my area of expertise.

But there is an even bigger legal threat on the horizon, especially for churches that preach unpopular (but traditional biblical) views of marriage and sexuality.[2] We have seen in recent years two similar sorts of online shaming and harassment. One is *doxxing*: mustering an online mob against someone, to make their life very unpleasant using means other than simply calling the police and accusing them of a crime. This has happened to individuals and small local establishments whose owners have expressed support for traditional views, for a while now (Brendan Eich, Masterpiece Cake Shop, etc.). But it can happen to churches and pastors as well.

A second kind of legal threat is posed by tech and financial services companies. Like most individuals and families, churches rely on websites and social media sites to share information (including streaming services). By now, everyone should be familiar with the pitfalls of sharing certain kinds of information on Facebook, Twitter, YouTube, etc., that does not fit the tech companies' vision of what should be said (either on marriage and sexuality, or religion, or COVID—see Chapter 13). Even more

---

2. Carl Trueman and Todd Pruitt, "Big Tech at the Church's Doorstep," *Mortification of Spin* podcast, 13 October 2021 <https://www.reformation21.org/blog/big-tech-at-the-churchs-doorstep>.

crucially, churches rely on banks and services like credit/debit cards, Paypal, Venmo, etc., for processing tithes and conducting the business of the church.

Whereas those companies had previously been neutral about serving all but the most extreme sorts of speech and organizations (child porn and the like), in recent years payment processors have been pressured by advocacy groups to stop serving certain…unpopular institutions. It starts like this: "Mastercard, Visa to block use of cards on Pornhub website"[3]—a development that traditional Christians might shortsightedly celebrate. But it next becomes this: "PayPal Partners with ADL to Fight Extremism and Protect Marginalized Communities."[4] Given the ever-expanding definition of "extremist and hate movements/speech," how long will it be before Christian churches, especially traditional ones, are included in this definition? Tech companies, prosecutors, and politicians can score popularity points by pressuring churches to change their messages, or be fined and shut down.

Even if, ultimately, freedom of speech and religious expression might be protected by courts (although this is becoming doubtful), the costs of legal defense and negative attention will be significant. Large churches might have the funds to fight these battles, but smaller churches will not. They will be forced to shut up or shut down, and the pastor and church trustees might face personal liability if sued.

In America at least, religious and political conservatives since the mid-twentieth century have traditionally been pro-market and pro-business (not the same thing), trusting the market rather than government to serve their interests. What conservatives need to learn from some on the old-school left, or left-anarchists, is

---

3. "Mastercard, Visa to block use of cards on Pornhub website," *CBS News*, December 11, 2020 <https://www.cbsnews.com/news/visa-mastercard-wont-allow-charges-pornhub/>.

4. *Anti-Defamation League*, 26 July 2021 <https://www.adl.org/resources/press-release/paypal-partners-adl-fight-extremism-and-protect-marginalized-communities>.

that corporations can be just as dangerous, especially when wed to the police power of the state. In many respects, the governance imposed by the five big tech companies (Google, Facebook/Instagram, Twitter/X, Microsoft, Amazon) is more relevant to how we live our lives than the governance of entities that exercise geographically-delineated monopolies on the legitimate use of force (i.e., "states"). Facebook may be the "tsar" that matters, more than the tsar himself—or the "tsar" will pressure Facebook to do its dirty work (see Chapter 13!).[5]

Wise as Serpents, Innocent as Doves, Bold as Lions

These issues might not seem connected at first glance. The overarching concern is about the erosion of the barrier between spheres of our lives due to communication technology. In the last two decades, most of us have slowly allowed more of our lives to slide into online space, for the sake of convenience and the amazing possibilities—and COVID lockdowns have only accelerated this for many of us. But the downside is that our individual selves, our families, and our communal lives have become more porous. Human existence requires boundaries, just as our skin protects the inside of our bodies.

The concerns about performativity, privacy, and scrutiny are linked by this idea of maintaining proper boundaries between the bodies who are part of the church and the rest of society. Just as the skin barrier that (imperfectly) protects a physical body is sometimes breached in a sterile, surgical theatre for the good of the body—so also the local church should reserve its space to be a hospital for human souls. This means protecting the privacy of the vulnerable who come to the hospital for spiritual surgery. It

---

5. Ignas Kalpokas, *Algorithmic Governance: Politics and Law in the Post-Human Era* (Cham, Switzerland: Palgrave Pivot, 2019).

could also mean more intentional efforts to respond to those who call for help in their homes (paramedics responding to emergency calls): visiting and ministering to those who are homebound (from whom "online church" can perhaps deflect our attention). Letting an unknown, broad, potentially-hostile online audience affect the church's reenactment of the divine drama of redemption (i.e., worship) is like letting the hospital's PR office dictate the mission, messaging, and priorities of the hospital organization: it may be useful for a hospital to do some broad public education about health matters, but the hospital's primary mission is treating the sick and injured.

On scrutiny: maintaining the proper boundary of the church also means clarifying and focusing our message to those outside the church. Churches should not hide what they teach; I appreciate when churches have clear doctrinal statements and confessions provided on their websites (and I am a bit wary of those that do not).

In 2014, there was a controversy when the first openly-lesbian mayor of the city of Houston, Annise Parker, demanded that Christian churches in Houston turn over to the mayor's office all their sermons and teachings about homosexuality and gender identity.[6] This demand is a totally improper overreach of state power into the realm of the church—and ultimately, it did not go anywhere legally. But if Mayor Parker's office were really interested in knowing what churches taught about homosexuality, gender identity, the gospel, or any other issue—they could have simply visited those churches' websites and watched or listened to their sermons (or perhaps visited the churches' Sunday services). I imagine that a large percentage of them post sermons or full services online. This means that the purpose was to shame these

---

6. Todd Starnes, "City of Houston demands pastors turn over sermons," *Fox News* opinion, Oct 14, 2014 <https://www.foxnews.com/opinion/city-of-houston-demands-pastors-turn-over-sermons>.

churches, not to actually investigate whether legitimately hateful things were being said at those churches.

I share Rod Dreher's assessment that churches cannot run from this forever. Soft persecution is coming, and it cannot be stopped in America or in Europe.[7] Churches cannot (and should not) hide their doctrines or shy away from taking biblical stands on important cultural issues. Churches will increasingly be challenged to defend their unpopular positions on things like marriage and gender identity. Anyone wishing to know the official beliefs of the denomination in which I am ordained as a minister, could chase that down online in a matter of minutes—I cannot hide from it, nor do I wish to hide my convictions.

But we can be wise about how and when we might endure this scrutiny when it comes. This means ensuring that only the gospel itself, and the core teachings of the Christian faith that stem from the gospel—not we ourselves through our imprudence—give offense (1 Pet 2:20). Pastors and elders, as individuals and speaking as councils who make statements on matters of import, are expected to be more measured and careful in our words than lay people. This means we should, in theory, be better prepared to stand up for the gospel when called to account for the words of the church.

I am not a lawyer, but it seems wise to create severable institutions that allow the church to persist even if individuals or local congregational leaders are subject to soft persecution. If the pastor is fined, sued, or arrested, or the church is shut down, the rest of the church should be able to continue on in a different form. My denomination has presbyterian church government; if one congregation in my presbytery is sued and has to close, that does not directly affect the other churches in the presbytery, which are

---

7. Rod Dreher, *Live Not By Lies: A Manual for Christian Dissidents* (New York: Sentinel, 2020).

legally independent entities. This legal firewall may contain the damage in such situations.

Conclusion

One solution for these issues, which I will develop further in Chapters 17 and 18, is to return to a situation in which only sermons are shared online, perhaps along with liturgy text, scripture, and songs prepared for home-bound worshipers.

Having only sermons online, subject to scrutiny, leaves the local church "on the hook" for only the official teaching of the church leaders—not off-the-cuff comments of a volunteer worship leader whose life might be ruined by doxxing, online shaming, or an overzealous, opportunistic prosecutor.

By placing sermons online, along with other liturgies for home worship, the church is compelled to renew our efforts to live with one another in physical presence, maintaining focus on one another. This means 1) resisting performativity when gathered for worship; 2) fostering appropriate privacy within the church community; 3) consistent visitation and care for those who cannot come to church for various reasons.

This is not an "inward turn" away from the world, but creating a safe haven for refugees from the world, and strengthening our secure home base (Christ, of course—but also his body, locally gathered) from which to be sent out as witnesses in the world.

PART II

A Plea for COVID Truth and Reconciliation in Christian Communities

Part I commends biblical ritual—including the sacraments, in-person worship, and in-person fellowship—as essential ways of "knowing" and experiencing God.

During the COVID crisis, churches and Christian communities could have been a haven for hurting and fearful people. Tragically, many churches fell short of this responsibility, in a variety of ways.

The root of the problem, I argue in Part II, is that many in the church failed to accept the foundational knowledge (epistemology) that God reveals to us in His Word, His rituals and His community. Instead, the church was, and continues to be, in thrall to the sources of knowledge and epistemologies of modernity. Course-correction is possible, however—that is the subject of Part III.

Truth and Repentance, Not Denial or Amnesty

Two statements should be uncontroversial. First, many churches in North America (or the West more broadly) are not doing well in the wake of the COVID-19 pandemic. This is due to a combination of many factors, most of which pre-dated the pandemic—but the pandemic accelerated many existing trends. Secondly, however, God is immensely pleased by genuine repentance (Luke 15:7, 10). I further expound this point from the book of Ezekiel specifically (Chapter 11), but this theme pervades every nearly book of the Old and New Testaments. God responds generously, graciously and mercifully to displays of genuine, heartfelt repentance. This applies both to individual repentance, and to corporate repentance led by community leaders.

The aim of Parts II and III is to commend individual and corporate repentance and reconciliation to Western Christian leaders in the wake of failures of response to the COVID-19 pandemic. These failures have left the church weak, divided, and compromised. There is a growing sense in the wider culture and in the church that "mistakes were made" (passive voice) during the pandemic, which can no longer be denied—but that "amnesty" should be granted to religious, political and scientific leaders so that society can put COVID behind us.[1]

I believe that, in order to move forward in faithfulness as healthy local expressions of the global, universal church, Christian leaders need to self-reflect, take accountability, and seek forgiveness and reconciliation. This involves publicly acknowledging failure and unfaithfulness in respect to three pandemic-related points, which I outline below.

In arguing for the need for a biblical "reckoning"—acknowledging the truth about what has transpired, seeking repentance and reconciliation—my goal is not to flagellate leaders or further tear down and divide churches. I grant that, in the midst of the pandemic, most pastors were trying desperately to preserve church unity *and* the lives of their congregants. It was a scary time, and knowledge about the virus was emerging (though not as quickly as it should have, as I will show in Chapters 12 and 13).

Rather, my message is similar to that of the prophet Haggai:

"You looked for much, and behold, it came to little. And when you brought it home, I blew it away. Why? declares the LORD of hosts. Because of my house that lies in ruins, while each of you busies himself with his own house. Therefore the heavens above you have withheld the dew, and the earth has withheld its produce. And I have called for a drought on the land and the hills, on the grain, the

---

1. See the calls for amnesty, and the adamant reactions against this notion in the following commentary: Emily Oster, "Let's Declare a Pandemic Amnesty," *The Atlantic*, 31 October 2022 <https://www.theatlantic.com/ideas/archive/2022/10/covid-response-forgiveness/671879/>; Michael Brendan Dougherty, "A 'Pandemic Amnesty'? Hell, No," *National Review*, 31 October 2022 <https://www.nationalreview.com/2022/10/a-pandemic-amnesty-hell-no/>; Paul D. Miller, "It's Time to Forgive Each Other Our Pandemic Sins," *Christianity Today*, 1 June 2023 <https://www.christianitytoday.com/2023/06/covid-19-pandemic-amnesty-masks-vaccine-lockdown-church/>.

new wine, the oil, on what the ground brings forth, on man and beast, and on all their labors." (Haggai 1:9–11)[2]

Our efforts to rebuild our struggling congregations have not been successful, in part because we have not dealt with these past failures to attend to YHWH's house. However, we serve a God who is "gracious and compassionate, slow to anger and abounding in loyalty-love," and who loves to respond to repentance with mercy. That is the gospel we preach, and it holds out the promise of renewal for churches, leaders and individuals who repent.

Three (Even Four) Grave Errors

Even though I have other opinions, the hills on which I choose to die with respect to worship and Christian community are these:

1) It is wrong to suspend in-person worship for extended periods of time. To do so robs Christian believers of necessary knowledge and experience of God's covenant love for them, and robs non-believers of a chance to hear and experience (intelligibly and fully) the good news of salvation in Jesus Christ. I immediately offer two caveats:

1a) I acknowledge that it is difficult to make a precise judgment as to "how long is too long"—who is to say that closing a church for five Sundays was acceptable, but six Sundays was too many? However, as with other ethical issues, the lack of a precise line does not render the principle invalid.

1b) I distinguish between making in-person worship *available* by keeping churches open, and *requiring or pressuring* all

---

2. See also my exegesis of this passage in Chapter 4 of Benjamin D. Giffone, *My Salvation Is Close At Hand: Isaiah 56–66 for the Church After Christendom* (Eugene, OR: Wipf & Stock, forthcoming).

members of a congregation to attend worship irrespective of conscience or health status.

2) It is wrong to segregate or exclude from in-person worship on the basis of health status, other than asking that sick people *voluntarily* stay home.

3) It is wrong to bind people's consciences on debatable issues and thereby add human-made laws to the law of God. In the pandemic, these debatable issues included masks, vaccines, and other mitigation measures, which were construed as "love of neighbor" and therefore a moral imperative. But construing only one single path as "love of neighbor," when all paths had costs and benefits to be weighed, constitutes an act of spiritual manipulation.

The second and third points will be explored in greater detail in Chapters 14–16. A fourth point is not a "hill to die on," but is rather a wisdom issue:

4) It is unwise and irresponsible for Christian leaders to abdicate major decisions to secular authorities who cannot be trusted to account for spiritual priorities according to Christian principles.

Please Read Before Burning

Thinking beyond the COVID era, a larger principle at stake is just how Christian leaders should relate to authorities: government authorities, medical authorities, scientific authorities, and the overall scientific project of modernity in which we live. Like Lucy holding the football for Charlie Brown, authorities have repeatedly taken advantage of church leaders' ignorance and well-meaning trust. At some point, however, Christian leaders must wise-up and rebuild a biblical view of the limits of scientific knowledge and governmental authority. The consequences are much more serious than Charlie Brown ending up on his back in the grass—people die spiritually, churches divide and compromise the gospel, and the church overall loses its "saltiness."

If you are a Christian leader, I urge you not to stop reading at this point, even if you think you do not need repentance for pandemic handling, or if you believe you will disagree with my points. You should regard this book as a resource for greater understanding between Christians—having read it, you will at least better understand those with whom you disagree. Furthermore, the pattern of acknowledgement, repentance and reconciliation can be applied to other church controversies, as well. Ultimately, we should draw wisdom from the scripture, including the book of Ezekiel, which is the frame for much of Part II.

CHAPTER 11 | A Survey of Leadership Texts in Ezekiel

One of several significant themes in Ezekiel is leadership: the importance of leaders to the life of the community, their failures and sins, and their (seemingly inexplicable) reinstatement in the eschatological vision of chapters 40–48. What follows is a non-exhaustive survey, in logical (rather than literary) order, to ground our considerations of church leadership in scripture—the development of one concept across a book of the canon.

Ezekiel is a priest and a prophet, and he is living at the twilight (or last days) of his country's independence. Judah has been attacked by the powerful Babylonian empire, and some of its people have been deported to Babylon. The temple of YHWH, the God of Israel, has not yet been destroyed; and the king still rules in Jerusalem—but only at the pleasure of the king of Babylon. Ezekiel was one of these exiles as a young adult in his 20s.

The Watchman (3:16–21; 33:1–9)

Ezekiel 3:16–21 sets forth an important task of a leader—in this case, a "watchman": to warn the people against wrongdoing and its consequences. If a leader knows the way of God and sees judgment coming, but does not warn the wicked, then the leader is partly responsible for that person's destruction ("his blood from your hand I will require"; 3:18). Ezekiel's vocation as a "watchman" in this fashion is renewed in 33:1–9.

The Shepherds (34)

Ezekiel 34:1–10 describes the leaders of Israel as faithless "shepherds of Israel" who have fattened and enriched themselves at the expense of the flock. Not only have they neglected the sheep so they are scattered (34:5–6), the shepherds have even slaughtered some of the sheep to eat (34:3). Especially poignant is the shepherds' failure to treat the sick, diseased, wounded and injured sheep under their care (34:4). In Ezekiel 34:20–22, the metaphor shifts somewhat to characterizing the leaders as "fat sheep" who have jostled and trampled the weaker sheep and excluded them from the feeding trough. As a result, YHWH says, "I am against the shepherds!" (34:10) In response, YHWH himself will shepherd and save his people (34:11–22), and will also send the Davidic messiah to be the single shepherd over them (34:23–34)—a powerful prefiguration of Jesus, the Good Shepherd (John 10), both fully human and fully God.

Corruption Behind Closed Doors (8–9)

Ezekiel 8–9 provides a powerful description of the corruption of the elites of Israel, both the religious leaders (priests and Levites) and the political leaders (king and elders). Ezekiel 8–9 is part of a vision that extends through chapter 11. From his home in Babylon, Ezekiel is carried in a vision to the temple in Jerusalem.

In something like "hidden-camera-style footage," Ezekiel is told to dig a peephole into the inner courts of the temple (8:7–8). He sees things that are done inside the temple by the religious and political elites of Israel. The elites are misusing a space that is sacred, given by YHWH for humans to access the transcendent, spiritual realm in only certain approved ways. The people of Israel and Judah trusted their priests, prophets and kings to do the necessary things in the sanctuary, according to the Law of Moses, that would lead to right relationship with their God and would result in safety and well-being for their society. But instead of communing with YHWH on behalf of the people, they are using it to contact other spirits and worship rebellious divine beings. They believe that YHWH does not see, that he is ignorant of what they are scheming/doing.

This idolatry is the culmination of a long decline of the priesthood. In the Old Testament, God gave tremendous responsibility to the Levitical priests: the knowledge of how the people could approach God. While some priests showed themselves worthy to minister, others abused their power and shielded themselves from criticism. Generations of priests came and went. Some were faithful, but many were corrupt. The priest whom Ezekiel sees in his vision (Shaphan, Ezek 8:11) was someone who *had* been from a family of righteous priest and scribes (2 Kgs 22:8–10; Jer 26:24), who had now entirely changed sides. The result is that rebel priests had led others astray, and had "filled the land with violence" (Ezek 8:17; 9:9–10). Rebellion against God never stops with "tolerance," but inevitably seeks to justify itself through controlling others, and/or simply to take money/sex (9:10; will to power).

The leaders tried to do all this corrupt worship behind closed doors, hiding it from the people. But Ezekiel knows—he had served as a priest and was probably aware of some of this corruption, but YHWH also gave him this prophetic vision. And, many of the common people know: it was likely an "open secret" in society that the leaders are not worshiping the God of Israel at all. In this case, the immediate solution is not reform, but destruction of this institution: kill people, defile the temple courts with the slain (9:7). Humans are not going to be able to reform or fix it at this late stage of decline. In only a few years, this temple will be torn down and these priests and leaders will be killed. The violence against these wicked people corresponds to the violence they have done upon others. However, it is carried out by God and his angels, not by the righteous remnant. God sometimes uses wicked people as His instrument to judge other wicked people; in this case, the wicked Babylonians will judge Judah's elites, but the Babylonians will themselves be judged by Judah's God.

There are a subset of laypeople who "sigh and groan at the abominations." These ones will be marked for salvation, with pen mark on their foreheads—like the houses marked with the blood of the lamb, at the Passover/exodus from Egypt.

Losing the Right to Appeal (20)

Ezekiel 16, 20 and 23 consist of lengthy, vivid narrations of the sins and failures of Israel and Judah to keep the covenant with YHWH. In a particularly harsh-but-honest moment: the elders of the exiles come to inquire of YHWH through Ezekiel, but YHWH responds incredulously, "Do you come to inquire of Me?! As I live, I will not be inquired of by you—utterance of Lord YHWH" (20:3). He then proceeds to accuse them ("Will *you* judge them? Will you judge, Son of Man?"; 20:4a) by narrating their idolatry going back all the way to their time in Egypt.[1] He concludes the narration by repeating: "As I live—utterance of Lord YHWH—I will not be inquired of by you!" (20:31d).

However, the passage concludes with a gracious promise: YHWH will not allow Israel and its leaders to remain languishing in the idolatrous life they have chosen and its punishment (20:32)—he will extract them from exile, purge the rebels from

---

1. For a discussion of the significance of this passage, see Benjamin D. Giffone, "'Anger Exhausted' for the Sake of YHWH's Name in Ezekiel 20: Did YHWH Really Relent from Wrath Poured Out on Israel?", *BZ* 66.1 (2022): 1–15.

their midst, and make them holy (20:33–38), for the sake of his name (20:39–44).

Repentance and Change of Trajectory (18:21–32; 33:10–20)

Ezekiel 18 describes how the generational cycle of sin can be broken, and children will not be held responsible for parents' sins (18:1–20). The emphasis then turns to directional repentance. Someone who turns from a lifetime of righteousness to do evil, trusting in his own righteousness, will not be delivered (18:24–26). But someone who turns from a lifetime of evil and lives a life of genuine repentance will be forgiven and live (18:21–23, 27–29). The accumulation of righteous deeds or sins matters less than the attitudes of arrogant self-righteousness or humble repentance. Following the renewal of Ezekiel's call as "watchman," Ezekiel 33:10–20 reemphasizes the importance of directional repentance, borrowing language from chapter 18.

Heart Transformation (36:22–32)

In a passage not specifically focused on leadership but nevertheless crucial to the gospel message of Ezekiel for leaders, Ezekiel 36:22–32 looks ahead to a day when the people of Israel will be rescued from exile and restored to relationship with YHWH, for the sake of His own reputation. The transformation of the hearts of the people is crucial to their restored, forgiven life as YHWH's people: "And I will give you a new heart, and a new spirit I will give within you; and I will remove the stone heart from your flesh, and I will give you a flesh heart; and my spirit I will give within you, and cause you to walk in my statutes, and my judgments you will keep and do" (36:26–27).[2]

---

2. See also Lev 26:40–44 and Deut 30:1–10, which use the image of "[un]circumcised heart."

Leadership Failures Erased? (44:4–31)

One of the most puzzling passages in Ezekiel from a purely historical perspective is Ezekiel 44, which occurs within the context of Ezekiel's New Temple Vision. In the envisioned future restoration, YHWH returns to his sanctuary and purifies it (Ezek 43:1–9), and then sets forth the requirements for how its purity should be maintained going forward (43:10–44:31), so that YHWH can have ongoing [eternal] fellowship with his people (48:35, "YHWH Is There").

In light of all that has come before in Ezekiel, it is not at all surprising to see a critique of the house of Israel (44:4–8) and the Levites (44:9–14) for failing to guard the purity of the sanctuary. The surprise is that the Zadoqite priests are commended and given exclusive charge of the sanctuary, because "they kept the charge of my sanctuary when the sons of Israel strayed from before me" (44:15; similar sentiments are found in 40:46 and 48:11). The descendants of Zadoq within the clan of Aaron had undoubtedly been part of the Jerusalem priesthood continuously from the time of David and Solomon (2 Sam 8:17; 1 Kgs 2:35; see prophecy in 1 Sam 2:35–36) until the exile (cf. 1 Chr 6:8–15 [MT 5:34–41]; 2 Chr 31:10; Ezr 7:2; Neh 11:11). In light of all the failures of the priesthood leading up to the exile, and the likely complicity of the Zadoqites in the unfaithfulness of the leadership of Israel, how can this commendation in 44:15 and 48:11 be true?

The tendency among biblical scholars is to see Ezekiel 44 as one of several voices in the Persian period advocating for different "ways forward" in the Second Temple community.[3] Whereas Ezekiel 44 excludes foreigners, Isaiah 56:1–8 and 66:21 allow that

---

3. See, among many others: Nathan MacDonald, *Priestly Rule: Polemic and Biblical Interpretation in Ezekiel 44* (BZAW 476; Berlin: de Gruyter, 2015); Benjamin Kilchör, "The Meaning of Ezekiel 44,6–14 in Light of Ezekiel 1–39," *Biblica* 98.2 (2017): 191–207, https://doi.org/10.2143/BIB.98.2.3217842.

foreigners may worship in the temple and even serve as priests and Levites. Whereas Ezekiel 44 condemns the Levites but commends the Zadoqite priests, the Chronicler alleges that the priests have been less scrupulous about personal and altar purity than were the Levites (2 Chr 29:34; 30:17–20, 22, 24; 31:17–18).[4]

Interpreting Ezekiel 44:15 and 48:11 canonically and in light of redemptive history, Christian readers can understand that the New Temple Vision finds its fulfillment in the person of Christ (the great High Priest) and in the church whom Christ would eventually sanctify for his priesthood (1 Pet 2:5, 9; Rev 1:6; 5:10). None of us is perfect on our own—yet through the imputation of Christ's righteousness and the continual sanctification by the Holy Spirit, we are considered righteous priests to the world despite our sins.[5]

Nevertheless, this reading sits in uneasy tension with the apparent historical reality that the Zadoqites get a pass and the Levites get thrown under the bus. This tension has implications for how we think about the continuity of religious authority through times of crisis and testing.

Summary

Spiritual and political leadership is important in Ezekiel. Even though each individual is responsible for his or her own choice to be loyal or disloyal to YHWH (18:2–4), leaders have power to influence the community in ways that lead to life or to disaster. Leaders "specialize" in doing the tasks of leadership that result in flourishing, survival, languishing or destruction for the people.

---

4. Jaeyoung Jeon, "The Levites and Idolatry: A Scribal Debate in Ezekiel 44 and Chronicles," in *Chronicles and the Priestly Literature of the Hebrew Bible*, ed. Louis Jonker and Jaeyoung Jeon, BZAW 528 (Berlin: de Gruyter, 2021), 348–374 <https://doi.org/10.1515/9783110707014-017>.

5. See the exposition of Zech 3:1–10 in Chapter 4 of Benjamin D. Giffone, *My Salvation Is Close At Hand: Isaiah 56–66 for the Church After Christendom* (Eugene, OR: Wipf & Stock, forthcoming).

Even if the laity do not see or have no control over what the leaders are doing, YHWH sees and will hold leaders accountable (Ezek 8–9; 34).

Unrepentant leaders cannot presume upon YHWH to appeal for help (Ezek 20). Yet even through community crises and failures of leadership, there is hope for leaders who repent (Ezek 33), receive a new heart (Ezek 36) and submit to the leadership of the Good Shepherd (Ezek 34). In the mystery of God's gracious plan, such repentant leaders can be regarded as faithful (Ezek 44) and lead God's people to flourishing life in fellowship with God himself (48:35).

CHAPTER 12

The Mistakes of Authorities During COVID

We now turn our attention to the painful and intricate task: describing the mistakes of public authorities during the COVID era. While it is impossible to catalogue these errors comprehensively (and more details are constantly emerging), it is necessary to provide a survey for the consideration of Christians reflecting back on this time.

While this section is not about the church per se, I will focus on errors that connect to three crucial issues affecting the church that I listed in Chapter 10. The first issue is extended church closures (beyond the initial few weeks). Meeting in person is necessary for at least two of the "means of grace": the sacraments,[1] and the fellowship of the saints (see Chapters 6 and 7). The second issue is the practice of segregating the church on the basis of health status. This amounts to a violation of the Galatians 2 principles of fellowship (see Chapter 14)—and, as we will see, this concession had no long-term effect on the spread of the virus. The third issue is coercion and manipulation with respect to issues that are matters of conscience and personal choice. On the part of religious leaders, this includes both the active use of the bully pulpit and

---

1. No doubt some in traditions other than my own (confessional Presbyterian) would balk at the term "sacrament," but I think the point is still clear: the Lord's Supper and Baptism cannot be done remotely.

the passive failure to defend individuals' freedom to act according to conscience (see Chapters 14 and 15).

This is not intended to be a book about science. I leave room for disagreement on many points—no doubt, every individual reader will have some disagreement with what I write here. Some readers will wish that I have been *more* aggressive, and others will wonder why I have chosen to be contrarian on a specific issue that was unnecessary.

To the extent that I highlight other issues, such as masks, vaccines, treatments, and natural immunity, it is in service of a meta-point: the secular authorities whom many Christian leaders trusted were wrong on nearly every point. In light of new revelations from the so-called "Twitter Files" and "Facebook Files," we now know that there was an illusion of consensus based on enforced conformity: scientific voices who expressed different opinions concerning the evidence were censored and threatened (further expounded in Chapter 13).

The 'Authorities' Were Wrong, Part I

In saying that the authorities were "wrong on every point," I mean that the general thrust of the advice given turned out to be incorrect, even if some individual scientific points were valid here and there.[2]

In this first list, I focus on points that were especially relevant for church life. Part II below adds a few additional errors that are notable even though they did not directly affect decisions made in Christian communities.

---

2. Marty Makary and Tracy Beth Høeg, "U.S. Public Health Agencies Aren't 'Following the Science,' Officials Say," *The Free Press*, 14 July 2022 <https://www.thefp.com/p/us-public-health-agencies-arent-following>.

Sanitization of Hands and Surfaces

It was known even by November 2020 that surface transmission of COVID was not a significant factor[3]—yet the CDC still recommended sanitation of hands and surfaces to prevent COVID as recently as late 2023.[4] Even publications that took the official pronouncements as reliable, such as *The Atlantic*, acknowledged in October 2022 that COVID was airborne and not preventable by handwashing and sanitizing surfaces.[5]

Distancing Requirements

Physical distancing (inexplicably and incorrectly dubbed "social distancing")[6] was perhaps the most significant principle of early mitigation efforts during the COVID-19 pandemic. Various governments required that individuals (other than family units) keep physical distance from one another in various settings, usually indoors but sometimes also outdoors.

This requirement had tremendous impact on capacity for many businesses, churches, and nearly all schools, where students

---

3. Mike Ives and Apoorva Mandavilli, "The Coronavirus Is Airborne Indoors. Why Are We Still Scrubbing Surfaces?" *The New York Times*, 18 November 2020 <https://www.nytimes.com/2020/11/18/world/asia/covid-cleaning.html>.

4. "To prevent the spread of germs during the COVID-19 pandemic, you should also wash your hands with soap and water for at least 20 seconds…" Centers for Disease Control, <https://www.cdc.gov/hygiene/personal-hygiene/hands.html> (accessed 27 November 2023).

5. Jacob Stern, "The Great Pandemic Hand-Washing Blooper," *The Atlantic*, 24 October 2024 <https://www.theatlantic.com/health/archive/2022/10/covid-pandemic-airborne-virus-transmission-hand-washing/671831/>

6. "Social distance" is a term from the field of sociology: "Refers to similarity or closeness based upon social variables measured on scales—as in some studies of occupational mobility, or in the Bogardus social distance scale. The latter measures social distance by the willingness to allow various ethnic groups to degrees of intimacy (for example, 'Would you accept a [Saudi Arabian] as a member of your golf club? … as a husband to your daughter?'). Methods of multi-dimensional scaling are often used to represent such social space and distance. The term is also used in network analysis to refer to the total number of links in the network that separate two individuals or groups." "Social Distance," in John Scott and Gordon Marshall, eds., *A Dictionary of Sociology*, 3rd ed. (New York: Oxford University Press, 2009), 700.

often sit close together and congregate in halls. The infeasibility of keeping individuals physically distanced from one another resulted in long-term closures or radical restructuring of spaces.

However, the distancing requirements were promulgated and vigorously enforced without rigorous testing, even years after the initial guidance. Some jurisdictions required a one-meter distance; others required two meters' distance (roughly equal to six feet); still others, a distance of one-and-a-half meters. In many settings, no accounting was made for ventilation or length of exposure. Years later, a key US government official offered no rigorous scientific basis for this disruptive requirement, admitting instead that the six-feet rule "sort of appeared."[7]

Age Stratification of Hospitalization/Death Risk

This was well understood by most people who had early experience with COVID, and was borne out in the earliest data. Healthy younger people are at a very low risk for bad outcomes from COVID, even in the initial variant (by many orders of magnitude).[8] Children especially were known to be at virtually no risk. Yet this issue was politicized, and the way that death totals were reported caused members of the public to radically overestimate their likelihood of being hospitalized from COVID.[9] A conflu-

7. Christian Britschgi, "Fauci to Congress: 6-Foot Social Distancing Guidance Likely Not Based on Data," *Reason*, 10 January 2024 <https://reason.com/2024/01/10/fauci-to-congress-6-foot-social-distancing-guidance-likely-not-based-on-data/>.

8. See the evidence marshaled by Bret Swanson, "How Did the Experts Turn Everything Upside Down?," *The Brownstone Institute*, 18 September 2023 <https://brownstone.org/articles/how-did-the-experts-turn-everything-upside-down/>. According to Ioannidis at al., October 2022, "The median IFR [infection fatality rate] was 0.0003% at 0–19 years, 0.002% at 20–29 years, 0.011% at 30–39 years, 0.035% at 40–49 years, 0.123% at 50–59 years, and 0.506% at 60–69 years. IFR increases approximately 4 times every 10 years." Ioannidis, J. P. A. et al., "Age-stratified infection fatality rate of COVID-19 in the non-elderly population," *Environmental research* 216(Pt 3), 114655 <https://doi.org/10.1016/j.envres.2022.114655>.

9. Jonathan Rothwell and Dan Witters, "U.S. Adults' Estimates of COVID-19 Hospitalization Risk," *Gallup Blog*, 27 September 2021 <https://news.gallup.com/opinion/gallup/354938/adults-estimates-covid-hospitalization-risk.aspx>.

ence of media sensationalism, government propaganda, and the well-known cognitive bias known as "the availability heuristic"[10] created a perfect storm that led to panic over the perceived danger to children, particularly in the USA. Schools in many states remained closed for nearly two years after the initial outbreak (long after many European countries had reopened primary schools, if they had ever closed them in the first place).

Masks

Masks became a flashpoint in all social settings, including churches. Cloth masks[11] and surgical masks[12] have been demonstrated to be largely ineffective against the spread of COVID, and this is consistent with what was known about the spread of aerosolized respiratory viruses at the time.[13] This is now acknowledged in academic studies and even published in corporate news

---

10. As defined and expounded in the work of Daniel Kahneman and Amos Tversky, for which Kahneman won a Nobel Prize in Economics (after Tversky passed away): "Kahneman and Tversky found that …the vast majority of people misestimate probabilities in predictable ways. …[One] bias Kahneman and Tversky found to be common in people's thinking is 'availability,' whereby people judge probabilities based on how available examples are to them. So, for example, people overstate the risk from driving without a seat belt if they personally know someone who was killed while driving without. Also, repetition of various stories in the news media, such as stories about children being killed by guns, causes people to overstate the risk of guns to children." David R. Henderson, "Daniel Kahneman," *Concise Encyclopedia of Economics*, n.d. <https://www.econlib.org/library/Enc/bios/Kahneman.html>.

11. Ian T. Liu, Vinay Prasad and Jonathan J. Darrow, "How Effective Are Cloth Face Masks? A summary of the scientific literature on the effectiveness of masking, both against respiratory infection generally and against COVID-19," *Regulation,* Winter 2021/2022 <https://www.cato.org/regulation/winter-2021/2022/how-effective-are-cloth-face-masks>.

12. Vinay Prasad, "A new mask randomized trial shows that masks work?" *Sensible Medicine* Substack, 25 July 2024 <https://www.sensible-med.com/p/a-new-mask-randomized-trial-shows>.

13. Eliza McGraw, "Everyone wore masks during the 1918 flu pandemic. They were useless," *The Washington Post*, 2 April 2020 <https://www.washingtonpost.com/history/2020/04/02/everyone-wore-masks-during-1918-flu-pandemic-they-were-useless/>; "Are Face Masks Effective? The Evidence," *Swiss Policy Research,* July 2020 (updated September 2023) <https://swprs.org/face-masks-evidence/>; Jenin Younes, "The Question of Masks," *American Institute for Economic Research*, 26 January 2021 <https://www.aier.org/article/the-question-of-masks/>; Jeffrey H. Anderson, "Do Masks Work? A review of the evidence," *City Journal*, 11 August 2021 <https://www.city-journal.org/article/do-masks-work>.

sources.[14] Yet the CDC continued to recommend them in schools long after they were proven ineffective,[15] and the use of surgical masks to contain respiratory viruses inexplicably persists in medical settings to this day (late 2024). Even N95 respirators are of limited value because they must be fitted properly, not touched/dirtied/compromised, and can only be warn properly for limited periods of time.[16]

Lockdowns and School Closures

Prior to 2020, lockdowns of healthy people to prevent transmission of a respiratory disease was not recommended by pandemic preparedness plans.[17] However, this became a preferred method of suppressing transmission, with some even hoping that the disease could be eradicated if we locked down long enough and severely enough. Other experts, notably those who drafted and signed the Great Barrington Declaration,[18] said that this was infeasible and unreasonable, and would result in other harms to vulnerable people (namely children, the working class, and the global

14. Mary Kay Linge, "Fauci admits to lack of COVID mask evidence—but wants us to wear them anyway," *New York Post*, 2 September 2023 <https://nypost.com/2023/09/02/fauci-admits-lack-of-covid-mask-evidence-but-still-wants-us-to-wear-them/>; Maryanne Demasi, "Lead Author of Cochrane Mask Review Responds to Fauci's Dismissal of Evidence," *The Daily Sceptic*, 09 September 2023 <https://dailysceptic.org/2023/09/09/lead-author-of-cochrane-mask-review-responds-to-faucis-dismissal-of-evidence/>.

15. David Zweig, "The CDC's Flawed Case for Wearing Masks in School," *The Atlantic*, 16 December 2021 <https://www.theatlantic.com/science/archive/2021/12/mask-guidelines-cdc-walensky/621035/>.

16. Vinay Prasad, "Should You Wear an N95/KN95/KF94? Should Kids in School?" *Vinay Prasad's Observations and Thoughts* Substack, 2 January 2022 <https://www.drvinayprasad.com/p/should-you-wear-an-n95kn95kn94>.

17. Micha Gartz, "What They Said about Lockdowns before 2020," *American Institute for Economic Research*, 13 January 2021 <https://www.aier.org/article/what-they-said-about-lockdowns-before-2020/>.

18. Martin Kulldorff, Sunetra Gupta, and Jay Bhattacharya, "The Great Barrington Declaration," October 4, 2020 <https://gbdeclaration.org/>.

poor).[19] Instead, they advocated focused protection so that older people could delay their encounter with the virus until vaccines and more effective treatments were available. While this could be the subject of many books, the result of the last five years is that nearly every person on the planet has had an encounter with one or more variants of this coronavirus. Once it was demonstrated that it could spread in animal populations,[20] it was hopeless to contain it. The experts who suggested early on that these facts should inform public health strategy were suppressed, censored, and ridiculed.

Outdoor Transmission

It was well-established early on that outdoor transmission of COVID was nearly impossible.[21] Getting exercise and sunlight (which causes the body to produce vitamin D) would have helped individuals encounter the COVID virus from a healthier baseline. Yet authorities closed playgrounds, beaches and parks to

---

19. "The Harms of Lockdowns, The Dangers of Censorship, And A Path Forward," *American Institute for Economic Research*, 12 April 2021 <https://www.aier.org/article/the-harms-of-lockdowns-the-dangers-of-censorship-and-a-path-forward/>; Angelo Codevilla, "The COVID Coup: And How to Unlock Ourselves," *The American Mind*, 17 July 2020 <https://americanmind.org/salvo/the-covid-coup/>.

20. For example, whitetail deer: "From April to December of last year [2020], about 30% of the deer that they tested were positive for SARS-CoV-2 by a PCR test. And then during the winter surge in Iowa, from Nov. 23, 2020, to Jan. 10 of this year [2021], about 80% of the deer that they tested were infected. At the peak of the surge, Kapur says, the prevalence of the virus in deer was effectively about 50 to 100 times the prevalence in Iowa residents at the time." Michaeleen Doucleff, "How SARS-CoV-2 in American deer could alter the course of the global pandemic," *NPR*, 10 November 2021 <https://www.npr.org/sections/goatsandsoda/2021/11/10/1054224204/how-sars-cov-2-in-american-deer-could-alter-the-course-of-the-global-pandemic>.

21. Peter Sullivan, "Evidence mounts that outside is safer when it comes to COVID-19," *The Hill*, 6 May 2020 <https://thehill.com/policy/healthcare/496483-evidence-mounts-that-outside-is-safer-when-it-comes-to-covid-19/>; Ronan McGreevy, "Outdoor transmission accounts for 0.1% of State's Covid-19 cases," *The Irish Times*, 05 April 2021 <https://www.irishtimes.com/news/ireland/irish-news/outdoor-transmission-accounts-for-0-1-of-state-s-covid-19-cases-1.4529036>; David E. Epperly, Kristopher R. Rinehart, David N. Caney, "COVID-19 Aerosolized Viral Loads, Environment, Ventilation, Masks, Exposure Time, Severity, And Immune Response: A Pragmatic Guide Of Estimates," medRxiv 2020.10.03.20206110; doi: https://doi.org/10.1101/2020.10.03.20206110

prevent people from congregating outside. Churches that tried to gather outside were sometimes broken up or punished.[22] Other churches did not try to gather outside for fear of punishment. In the Summer of 2020, however, Black Lives Matter protests were encouraged despite the risk of COVID transmission, because systemic racism was deemed a "public health emergency."[23] This inconsistency eroded trust in public health authorities.

Asymptomatic Transmission

The historic approach to infectious disease has been for sick people to stay away from others to avoid infecting them. Many outward symptoms of infectious disease (sneezing, coughing, diarrhea, etc.) are themselves typically the means of transmission. Symptoms were a sign of contagiousness.

One rationale for requiring non-pharmaceutical interventions (NPI) such as masks or handwashing to slow or halt the spread of COVID was that people who were not apparently sick (i.e., they have no symptoms) could nevertheless be infected and infectious—so-called asymptomatic or presymptomatic spread. In this view, anyone could become a carrier of the disease without knowing it.

As early as 2020, it was acknowledged by health authorities such as the WHO that asymptomatic spread of COVID was

22. Michelle Boorstein, "Federal court allows D.C. church to hold services outdoors despite coronavirus restrictions," *The Washington Post*, 10 October 2020 <https://www.washingtonpost.com/religion/2020/10/10/judge-approves-dc-church-coronavirus-challenge-mayor-bowser/>; Clare Hymes, "U.S. Justice Department backs church in dispute over city ban on drive-in services," *CBS News*, 14 April 2020 <https://www.cbsnews.com/news/justice-department-church-greenville-mississippi-coronavirus-order/>.

23. Tara Haelle, "Risking Their Lives To Save Their Lives: Why Public Health Experts Support Black Lives Matter Protests," *Forbes*, 20 June 2020, <https://www.forbes.com/sites/tarahaelle/2020/06/19/risking-their-lives-to-save-their-lives-why-public-health-experts-support-black-lives-matter-protests/>.

rare.[24] One early study found that the secondary attack rate within households (i.e., close contact) of asymptomatic individuals was only 0.7%, versus 18% for a symptomatic infected person.[25]

The logical implication for this would be a policy/messaging approach of, "If you're sick, stay home," and perhaps financially incentivizing low-income or gig-economy workers to take off from work if they have symptoms. Churches could have taken this approach. Yet authorities cultivated an illusion that every person was an equal threat to everyone else, an approach with significant consequences for social behavior and moral perception (see Chapter 14).

Natural (Infection-Acquired) Immunity

It is abundantly clear that COVID infection confers a lasting immunity that makes contracting COVID again much less likely, and greatly lessens the severity of the disease if contracted again.[26] This is consistent with nearly all human experience with disease throughout recorded history.

24. Jeffrey Tucker, "Asymptomatic Spread Revisited," *American Institute for Economic Research*, 22 November 2020 <https://www.aier.org/article/asymptomatic-spread-revisited/>; Cao, S., Gan, Y., Wang, C. et al., "Post-lockdown SARS-CoV-2 nucleic acid screening in nearly ten million residents of Wuhan, China," *Nat Commun* 11, 5917 (2020), <https://doi.org/10.1038/s41467-020-19802-w>; Will Feuer and Noah Higgins-Dunn, "Asymptomatic spread of coronavirus is 'very rare,' WHO says," *CNBC*, 8 Jun 2020 <https://www.cnbc.com/2020/06/08/asymptomatic-coronavirus-patients-arent-spreading-new-infections-who-says.html>.

25. Lexie Pitzen, "Asymptomatic COVID Spread Unlikely but Possible, According to Study," *Tallahassee Reports*, 31 December, 2020 <https://tallahasseereports.com/2020/12/31/asymptomatic-covid-spread-unlikely-but-possible-according-to-study/>.

26. V. Hall et al., "Do antibody positive healthcare workers have lower SARS-CoV-2 infection rates than antibody negative healthcare workers? Large multi-centre prospective cohort study (the SIREN study), England: June to November 2020," medRxiv 2021.01.13.21249642; doi: https://doi.org/10.1101/2021.01.13.21249642; "COVID-19 survivors may possess wide-ranging resistance to the disease," *Emory News Center*, 22 July 2021 <https://news.emory.edu/stories/2021/07/covid_survivors_resistance/index.html>.

Interestingly, it was mainly USA authorities who got this one wrong.[27] My own story living in Europe until mid-2022 is illustrative. I was initially quite hopeful about vaccines, but undecided about whether to take them when they were developed. My ten years working in the pharma industry taught me that the majority of promising treatments do not work as intended—in fact, most treatments end up being dead-ends. My family ended up contracting COVID in late 2020, before vaccines were even available anywhere. This made the vaccine question moot for me and my family: it made no sense to get vaccinated against an illness from which one has already recovered.[28] In many European countries, even those that later had strict vaccine mandates and programs of social segregation, the "immunity" requirements included a provision for those who had recovered from COVID. Recovery from COVID could be registered by a positive PCR test or an antibody test.[29] Research has subsequently demonstrated the vast superiority of natural immunity over vaccines as protection against bad outcomes from subsequent infections.[30]

27. Jennifer Block, "Vaccinating people who have had covid-19: why doesn't natural immunity count in the US?" *BMJ* 2021; 374 :n2101 doi:10.1136/bmj.n2101 <https://doi.org/10.1136/bmj.n2101>.

28. Paul Alexander, "If You Had Covid, Do You Need the Vaccine?" *American Institute for Economic Research*, 6 April 2021 <https://www.aier.org/article/if-you-had-covid-do-you-need-the-vaccine/>.

29. Though, it should be pointed out that these tests were unreliable and had different thresholds required for the recoveree to be counted as "immune"; this was my own experience and that of several others who sought regular testing—we all "shopped around" for the labs that would give us the best results, and measured antibody counts varied widely, even on consecutive days. See Giedrė Skridailaitė, "Skirtingose laboratorijose gali skirtis antikūnų tyrimų rezultatai – ministerija spragą žada ištaisyti" ("The Results of Antibody Tests—Ministry Promises to Fix the Gap in Different Laboratories"), *LRT* (Lithuanian), 25 October 2021 <https://www.lrt.lt/naujienos/sveikata/682/1527998/skirtingose-laboratorijose-gali-skirtis-antikunu-tyrimu-rezultatai-ministerija-spraga-zada-istaisyti>.

30. Jeffrey A. Tucker, "The World Health Organization Oversold the Vaccine and Deprecated Natural Immunity," *The Brownstone Institute*, 29 August 2021 <https://brownstone.org/articles/the-world-health-organization-oversold-the-vaccine-and-deprecated-natural-immunity/>; "'Bombshell' study finds natural immunity superior to vaccination," *UnHerd*, 26 August 2021 <https://unherd.com/newsroom/bombshell-study-finds-natural-immunity-superior-to-vaccination>

When American authorities made no such distinction and tried to compel those who had recovered from COVID to be vaccinated, trust in the vaccine was undermined.[31] Many people rightly interpreted the pressure to get vaccinated as serving some greater bureaucratic plan that was not communicated, rather than their well-being. Tens of thousands of Americans were terminated from their jobs,[32] expelled from the military[33] or the medical professions,[34] because natural immunity was not recognized.

Many of these Americans did not receive moral or financial support from their Christian communities because of their choice, only silence—or worse: ridicule and scorn. Church leaders that tried to segregate or pressure into vaccination those who recovered from COVID on the basis of "controlling transmission" were factually incorrect (see below) and morally wrong, and thereby did damage to those people who had recovered (the physical risk of vaccination after COVID recovery; or the damage to their consciences, souls, or livelihoods).

Vaccine Efficacy in Controlling Transmission

The hypothetical use of vaccines to control transmission (a so-called "sterilizing vaccine") would be the only valid rationale for requiring vaccines or segregating churches (though coercion

---

31. Jeffrey A. Tucker, "How Coercion Compromised the Vaccine," *The Brownstone Institute*, 28 March 2022 <https://brownstone.org/articles/how-coercion-compromised-the-vaccine/>.

32. Adeola Adeosun, "Woman Fired For Refusing Covid Vaccine Wins Record $12 Million," *Newsweek*, 09 November 2024 <https://www.newsweek.com/woman-fired-refusing-covid-vaccine-wins-record-millions-1983294>.

33. Kenneth Niemeyer, "The US Army is having a hard time recruiting. Now it's asking soldiers dismissed for refusing the COVID-19 vaccine to come back," *Business Insider*, 18 November 2023 <https://www.businessinsider.com/us-army-invites-back-vaccine-refusing-soldiers-amid-recruitment-crisis-2023-11>.

34. Laura Newberry, "UC Irvine fires physician who refused to get vaccinated, claiming 'natural immunity,'" *Los Angeles Times*, 2 January 2022 <https://www.latimes.com/california/story/2022-01-02/uc-irvine-fires-physician-who-refused-to-get-vaccinated-claiming-natural-immunity>.

should still be rejected on principle). But the vaccines proved to be ineffective at controlling transmission—nearly everyone has now contracted COVID, whether unvaccinated, previously vaccinated, or even "boosted."[35] Most people who received a vaccine also got COVID, either within the early window of a few weeks when immune response is suppressed, or after the virus evolves and protection wears off.

In August of 2022, the CDC's own publication, *MMWR*, stated: "Receipt of a primary series alone, in the absence of being up to date with vaccination through receipt of all recommended booster doses, provides minimal protection against infection and transmission. Being up to date with vaccination provides a transient period of increased protection against infection and transmission after the most recent dose, although protection can wane over time."[36]

The initial claims in late 2020 and early 2021 by authorities about vaccinees being a "dead-end" for virus transmission, were incorrect.[37] Thus, vaccination may have benefits for the individual, but cannot be understood as an imperative of "neighbor-love."

35. Steven Li, "COVID-19 Outbreak in Israel, Fully Vaccinated Individuals Make Up 50% of Infected Adults," *Vision Times*, 30 June 2021 <https://www.visiontimes.com/2021/06/30/covid-19-israel-full-vaccinated.html>; "Vaccinated People Also Spread the Delta Variant, Yearlong Study Shows," *Bloomberg*, 28 October 2021 <https://www.bloomberg.com/news/articles/2021-10-28/getting-vaccinated-doesn-t-stop-people-from-spreading-delta>.

36. G.M. Massetti et al., "Summary of Guidance for Minimizing the Impact of COVID-19 on Individual Persons, Communities, and Health Care Systems—United States, August 2022," *MMWR Morb Mortal Wkly Rep* 2022;71:1057-1064. DOI: http://dx.doi.org/10.15585/mmwr.mm7133e1

37. In April 2024, Finnish reporter Ike Novikoff reported (<https://twitter.com/ikenovikoff/status/1778447143314849864>) the testimony of Dr. Hanna Nohynek, chief physician at the Finnish Institute for Health and Welfare and serves as the WHO's chair of Strategic Group of Experts on immunization. Dr. Nohynek testified that the Finnish Institute for Health knew by the summer of 2021 that the COVID-19 vaccines did not stop virus transmission, yet Finland and the EU continued the July–August 2021 rollout of the EU Digital COVID Certificate Regulation (to which I myself was subject as a resident of the EU member state of Lithuania at the time).
See also: Holmes Lybrand, "Fact check: Four times Walensky's comments were out of step with CDC guidance," *CNN*, 21 May 2021 <https://www.cnn.com/2021/05/21/politics/walensky-comments-cdc-guidance-fact-check/index.html>; Will Jones, "Vaccine Passports Make No Sense as the Vaccinated Are More Likely to Be Infected, Scientists Tell MPs," *The Daily Sceptic*, 22 November 2021 <https://dailysceptic.org/2021/11/22/vaccine-passports-make-no-sense-as-the-

Some may argue (without evidence) that the vaccine *could* have eliminated the original strain if everyone had taken the vaccines before the virus had a chance to mutate. But even if the vaccines could have controlled transmission initially, a plan that would have required nearly 8 billion people to be vaccinated in a short period of time (before significant evolution of the virus) was not practically feasible.[38]

Vaccine Safety and Risks

The COVID-19 vaccines were commended by authorities as "safe and effective," but both adjectives represent an oversimplification— the important considerations are *relative*: safety *compared to risks* of infection and side-effects, and effectiveness *compared to* placebo or other treatments.

As noted in the previous subsection, the vaccines were not effective at preventing infection. It is now also widely acknowledged that mild side-effects of the vaccines are widespread, and moderate-to-severe side-effects are roughly 1-in-800 per shot (see "Excursus: On Vaccines" below).[39] The authorities were wrong to

---

vaccinated-are-more-likely-to-be-infected-scientists-tell-mps/>; Paul Elias Alexander, "Extensive Efficacy Studies that Rebuke Vaccine Mandates," *The Brownstone Institute*, 28 October 2021 <https://brownstone.org/articles/16-studies-on-vaccine-efficacy/>; Vinay Prasad, "Vaccine effectiveness (against infection not severe disease) goes down the drain: Plummeting VE changes health care policy," *Vinay Prasad's Observations and Thoughts* Substack, 9 January 2022 <https://www.drvinayprasad.com/p/vaccine-effectiveness-goes-down-the>.

38. Herb Scribner, "The delta variant could evade vaccines if it becomes Delta 4+, new paper warns," *Deseret News*, 26 August 2021 <https://www.deseret.com/coronavirus/2021/8/26/22642809/delta-variant-evade-vaccines-mutations/>; Lisa M. Krieger, "New UCSF study: Vaccine-resistant viruses are driving 'breakthrough' COVID infections," *The Mercury News*, 30 August 2021 <https://www.mercurynews.com/2021/08/27/new-ucsf-study-vaccine-resistant-viruses-are-driving-breakthrough-covid-infections/>.

39. Robert M. Kaplan and Sander Greenland, "Why We Question the Safety Profile of mRNA COVID-19 Vaccines," *Sensible Medicine* Substack, 14 September 2022 <https://www.sensible-med.com/p/why-we-question-the-safety-of-covid>.

characterize the COVID-19 vaccines as "safe," especially compared to other previously-approved vaccines.[40]

Ethics of Vaccine Development, Testing and Production

Many Christians (and some non-Christians) were interested in COVID-19 vaccinations, but had concerns about whether the development, testing or production of the new vaccine products were dependent on fetal stem cells or other practices thought to be unethical. The rapid development of these products, the lack of transparency, and the immediate pressure to take vaccines as a way out of the pandemic exacerbated people's concerns. Pastors and Christian leaders should have been demanding greater transparency and more time to assess the claims made by manufacturers,[41] so Christians with concerns could have those allayed.[42]

I advocated in my Christian academic institution that accommodations be made to allow students who did not want to take the vaccine on ethical grounds, to continue to study online (our country mandated that all in-person students meet the "immunity pass" [the Orwellian-termed "opportunity pass"] requirements). Those students' pleas were denied by our administration, and the students had to take leave of absence or get vaccinated (or contract COVID, as nearly all eventually did by the omicron-variant

---

40. Joseph A. Ladapo and Harvey A. Risch, "Are Covid Vaccines Riskier Than Advertised? There are concerning trends on blood clots and low platelets, not that the authorities will tell you," *WSJ Opinion*, 22 June 2021 <https://www.wsj.com/articles/are-covid-vaccines-riskier-than-advertised-11624381749>.

41. Some Christian institutions were pressing governments and companies for more information regarding the use of various development and testing procedures: David Prentice and Tara Sander Lee, "What you need to know about the COVID-19 vaccines," *Charlotte Lozier Institute*, 8 December 2020, updated 2 June 2021 <https://lozierinstitute.org/what-you-need-to-know-about-the-covid-19-vaccine/>.

42. And this does not even include concerns about the ethics and integrity of the testing process and data; see Paul D. Thacker, "Covid-19: Researcher blows the whistle on data integrity issues in Pfizer's vaccine trial," *BMJ* 2021; 375 :n2635 doi:10.1136/bmj.n2635.

wave of February 2022—including vaccinated students and staff). I share this story in more detail in Chapter 14.

The 'Authorities' Were Wrong, Part II

The following issues were not directly related to church life or decisions that needed to be made within Christian communities, but nevertheless demonstrate the ineptness (or unwillingness) of authorities to rationally adjust to evidence that would have affected policy and behaviors.

Origins of the Virus

Was the SARS-COV-2 virus of natural zoonotic origin, or the product (accidental or intentional) of dangerous gain-of-function research? While this is not directly relevant to the life of the church, it goes to the lack of transparency and the possible recklessness of public officials in funding dangerous research.[43] Furthermore, zoonotic versus gain-of-function origin of the virus affected scientific models of how the virus might evolve, whether it could jump to other animals (rendering a vaccination solution unlikely), and how much evolutionary "tension" was built up, waiting to unwind in other variants. Early on, the natural (zoonotic) origin hypothesis was advanced as the most likely, by officials who had a professional (and legal) interest in covering up dangerous research. At some point, it became not "racist" but acceptable to consider a possible "lab leak" or gain-of-function origin of the virus.[44] Since Christians should oppose racism and xenophobia

43. Christian Britschgi, "Should We Blame Fauci for the COVID Pandemic?" *Reason*, 14 September 2024 <https://reason.com/2024/09/14/faucis-pandemic/>.

44. Robby Soave, "Lab Leak Is Not a Conspiracy Theory, Anthony Fauci Concedes," *Reason* 10 January 2024 <https://reason.com/2024/01/10/lab-leak-is-not-a-conspiracy-theory-anthony-fauci-concedes/>.

but should support government transparency, this is an important issue. It also goes to the trustworthiness of the authorities who were making pronouncements on both the origins of the virus and mitigation measures.

Early Treatments

The most popularly discussed off-patent, off-label early treatments for COVID are hydroxychloroquine and ivermectin.[45] These drugs have seemed to be effective for some COVID patients, but this is a very controversial topic with trial data and studies pointing in different directions. Regardless of the efficacy, however, there is no disputing that these drugs are *safe* when prescribed at normal doses for humans, by doctors.[46] So-called "off-label" use of FDA-approved drugs is common, as doctors use existing approved medications for new situations.[47] Yet these drugs were smeared (in some countries) as veterinary medicine, unsafe for humans.[48] Doctors who prescribed these medicines had

---

45. Justus R. Hope, "India's Ivermectin Blackout," *The Desert Review* (opinion), 9 August 2021 <https://www.thedesertreview.com/opinion/columnists/indias-ivermectin-blackout/article_e3db8f46-f942-11eb-9eea-77d5e2519364.html>; Charles L. Hooper and David R. Henderson, "The FDA's War Against the Truth on Ivermectin," *American Institute for Economic Research*, 18 October 2021 <https://www.aier.org/article/the-fdas-war-against-the-truth-on-ivermectin/>.

46. A *Nature* article from 2017 called ivermectin "extraordinary" and "a wonder drug": "Ivermectin has now been used for over three decades to treat parasitic infections in mammals, and has an extremely good safety profile, with numerous studies reporting low rates of adverse events when given as an oral treatment for parasitic infections. Several problematic reactions have been recorded, but they are generally mild and usually do not necessitate discontinuation of the drug." Andy Crump, "Ivermectin: enigmatic multifaceted 'wonder' drug continues to surprise and exceed expectations," *Journal of Antibiotics* 70 (2017): 495–505 <https://doi.org/10.1038/ja.2017.11>.

47. "Experimental/compassionate use" refers to the use of unapproved treatments for dying patients who cannot wait for the lengthy testing and approval process (also called the "right to try"). "Off-label" refers to the use of drugs that are safe and approved, to treat illnesses for which they are not (yet) indicated. "Off-patent" refers to drugs/treatments that are approved but the patent has expired, meaning that anyone is free to manufacture them (so they are no longer profitable for the company that held the patent).

48. David R. Henderson and Charles L. Hooper, "Why Is the FDA Attacking a Safe, Effective Drug? Ivermectin is a promising Covid treatment and prophylaxis, but the agency is denigrating it," *WSJ Opinion*, 28 July 2021 <https://www.wsj.com/articles/fda-ivermectin-covid-19-coronavirus-masks-anti-science-11627482393>.

their licenses threatened, and some pharmacists were afraid to fill prescriptions.[49] From a Christian perspective that values freedom and general humility in light of all that is not known about the wonders of the human body, doctors should have been free to prescribe FDA-approved medications "off-label" for treating COVID (with informed consent of the patient).

Excursus: On Vaccines

No doubt there will be readers of this chapter who wish me to be more emphatic in my opposition to COVID vaccines, or to emphasize all of the risks, side effects, and adverse events in my comments. I am choosing not to do so, for several reasons.

This is a very complicated issue. Even though I have worked adjacent to clinical research (ten years in pharma, processing regulatory and trial documentation), I am not a scientist. Various COVID vaccines have different mechanisms of action, efficacy, and safety/risk profiles. Ultimately, the precise safety profile of specific vaccines is not relevant to the question of whether people should have been compelled to take them or segregated/penalized on the basis of not taking them.

(I do address the efficacy of the vaccines at preventing infection and transmission, because this was an important reason given for requiring or compelling vaccination. One may still argue that even a "sterilizing" vaccine [i.e., one that completely prevents infection and transmission] should not be compulsory, on the grounds of personal medical freedom. However, everyone should agree that a *non-sterilizing* vaccine cannot be made compulsory; even if the vaccine improves the outcomes for the vaccinee who

---

49. Connor Walcott, "FDA Lawyer Announces Ivermectin Can be Prescribed for COVID-19," *Valuetainment,* 11 August 2023 <https://valuetainment.com/fda-lawyer-announces-ivermectin-can-be-prescribed-for-covid-19/>

contracts the disease, the decision to receive or to decline the vaccine only affects the vaccinee.)

The side effects and adverse events of vaccines are real questions, and I have found that it is difficult for those who willingly took the vaccine and suffered no apparent ill effects (this is the case for the vast majority of vaccinees, as far as is known at the end of 2024), to accept that others might have made a different choice in good faith. After all, those who willingly took the vaccine believed it was a good thing for them, and most believed it was good for others as well. It is difficult for "willing-and-eager" vaccinees to empathize with those who were hesitant. It is also hard for "willing-and-eager" vaccinees who suffered no/mild/temporary side effects to empathize with those who are vaccine-injured.[50] It is even difficult for those who may have been vaccine-injured to entertain the notion that the vaccine is the cause of their suffering.[51]

I am asking church leaders who were "willing" vaccinees to put themselves in the shoes of those who were hesitant for reasons that the leaders did not find compelling, and to acknowledge the following:

1) It turns out side effects and adverse events are real, and more frequent than with other vaccines.[52]

---

50. The website www.realnotrare.com allows people to share their COVID vaccine injury stories.

51. Moreover, systematic censorship (see Chapter 13) of vaccine-injury mutual support groups on Facebook and other platforms made difficult for suffering individuals to compare symptoms and explore possible treatments, leading to further emotional suffering (isolation, hopelessness) and physical suffering (missing out on potential treatments).

52. Current meta-analyses place the chance of serious adverse events from the mRNA COVID vaccines (Pfizer/BioNTech and Moderna) at roughly 1-in-800 per shot (so, 1-in-400 for a two-shot initial series). This risk is far greater than the risks of harm for other vaccines. Peter Doshi, "Covid-19: Researchers face wait for patient level data from Pfizer and Moderna vaccine trials," *BMJ* 2022; 378 doi: https://doi.org/10.1136/bmj.o1731 (Published 12 July 2022); Joseph Fraiman et al., "Serious adverse events of special interest following mRNA COVID-19 vaccination in randomized trials in adults," *Vaccine* 40:40 (22 September 2022), 5798–5805 <https://doi.org/10.1016/j.vaccine.2022.08.036>; Jay Bhattacharya, "Study into mRNA vaccine death rates sends 'danger signals,'" *UnHerd*, 3 May 2022 <https://unherd.com/newsroom/study-into-mrna/>; Jason Gale, "Largest Covid Vaccine Study Yet Finds Links to Health Conditions," *Bloomberg* 19 February 2024 <https://www.bloomberg.com/news/articles/2024-02-19/largest-covid-vaccine-study-yet-finds-links-to-health-conditions>.

2) The vaccines were not effective at stopping transmission (see above).

3) The highest public authorities who offered assurances that the vaccines were "safe and effective" at stopping contraction, transmission and death knew at the time that there were serious questions about effectiveness, if not safety as well.[53]

4) Well-known voices spoke up at the time to say that authorities *could not have known* without longer testing that the vaccines were actually safe and effective. Those voices were censored (see Chapter 13), but their concerns (which turned out to be justified) completely undermine the basis for compulsory vaccination.

I do not wish to litigate the question or the specific details of the claims. All I wish is for those who took the vaccine willingly, probably the majority of people reading this book, to recognize that the vaccine-hesitant had legitimate concerns at the time—concerns which have now been borne out—and to note that government authorities proved themselves untrustworthy in these matters. Going forward, Christian leaders should demand medical freedom and stand up against discrimination or compulsion.[54] Those who believe they have been vaccine-injured should be compensated if their claims are valid.[55]

---

53. Zachary Stieber, "CDC Director Admits Agency Gave False Information on COVID-19 Vaccine Safety Monitoring," *The Epoch Times*, 13 September 2022 <https://www.theepochtimes.com/article/cdc-director-admits-agency-gave-false-information-on-covid-19-vaccine-safety-monitoring-4726981>.

54. Jeffrey A. Tucker, "How Coercion Compromised the Vaccine," *The Brownstone Institute*, 28 March 2022 <https://brownstone.org/articles/how-coercion-compromised-the-vaccine/>.

55. Christian Britschgi, "COVID Vaccine Injuries Deserve a Day in Court," *Reason*, 12 February 2024 <https://reason.com/2024/02/12/covid-vaccine-injuries-deserve-a-day-in-court/>

Ultimately, Everyone Got COVID

Even those who disagree with the strongest statements I have made that "the authorities were wrong," must acknowledge that in the end, nearly everyone got COVID—with variants circulating, most have now contracted SARS-COV-2 multiple times.[56]

(This idea that nearly everyone would get the disease is implied in the frequently-employed phrase, "flatten the curve." The idea was to prevent high peaks in the temporal "curve" of infections that could threaten to overwhelm hospitals. But the area under the curve—the total number of people who would be infected—would not change meaningfully; this was understood from previous epidemics of respiratory viruses. Somehow, "flatten the curve" evolved into a belief [fostered by authorities] that the infection could be fully avoided, perhaps with the advent of a hoped-for sterilizing vaccine—thereby "crushing the curve.")

Thus, as we look back on things we did (lockdowns, masks, washing, distancing,[57] vaccine requirements), none of them actually made a meaningful change in the course of the pandemic—it is doubtful that these interventions would have prevented people from getting sick with COVID.[58] It is conceivable that "focused protection" and testing in nursing homes would have delayed infection of vulnerable people until effective vaccines or treatments were developed. Because the lockdown measures in certain places were so drastic and wide-ranging, they were unsustainable and

56. Aria Bendix, "People who've had Covid at least 5 times describe how the illness changed with each reinfection," *NBC News*, 8 October 2023 <https://www.nbcnews.com/health/health-news/covid-5-times-people-describe-illnesses-rcna118132>.

57. Josh Christenson, "COVID '6-feet' social distancing 'sort of just appeared,' likely lacked scientific basis, Fauci admits," *New York Post*, 10 January 2024 <https://nypost.com/2024/01/10/news/fauci-admits-to-congress-that-certain-covid-social-distancing-guidelines-lacked-scientific-basis-sort-of-just-appeared/>

58. Virginia Hume, "Our Failed COVID Response: If, God forbid, we face another pandemic, we cannot use our COVID strategy as the baseline," *The Dispatch* Substack, 22 April 2022 <https://thedispatch.com/article/our-failed-covid-response/>.

costly for all—whereas more targeted measures might have been maintainable for longer. But this is unknowable, as even the Great Barrington Declaration drafters must now admit.[59]

In this light, we look back and recognize that some of the preventative measures may have given misguided people a false sense of security. In an environment of fear, they were perceived as pastorally necessary in order to maintain the peace of many congregations. I would say that it was worthwhile to restructure worship to a certain degree for the sake of peace and corporate worship, but we must in retrospect recognize that they were not necessary or effective.

During the winter months of the pandemic years, our little church in Lithuania moved from the small upper room we rented in another church's building, to the main sanctuary, so that we could spread out (we had to change the time of our worship service and increase our rent payment in order to use this space). When serving communion, I wore a mask, and visibly used hand sanitizer[60] before touching anything. I believed at the time that these measures were of little or no value in preventing the spread of COVID. But I did them so that fearful people would not hesitate to come forward to be blessed by my administration of the means of grace. Also, I was not certain that I was correct, and I did not feel that those interventions were worth breaking fellowship over.

But ultimately, those things objectively did not do anything to prevent people from getting COVID in the long run.

---

59. Kevin Bardosh et al., "The unintended consequences of COVID-19 vaccine policy: why mandates, passports and restrictions may cause more harm than good," *BMJ Global Health* 2022;7:e008684 <https://doi.org/10.1136/bmjgh-2022-008684>.

60. I am personally a big believer in hand hygiene for the prevention of other illnesses. I am such a fan that I dragged my family on our Summer 2022 Budapest visit to the street named after Ignaz Semmelweis, the nineteenth-century physician who, despite being ridiculed by colleagues, promoted handwashing, and is today called "The Savior of [Expectant] Mothers." But it is evident that handwashing has little effect on COVID transmission.

CHAPTER 13 | Censorship, Propaganda, and The Illusion of Consensus

It might be tempting for some readers to attribute all of the errors chronicled in the previous chapter to incompetence, lack of communication between scientific and political elites, and the "fog of war"—rather than malice or willful ignorance and manipulation. Absent solid evidence of conspiracy, incompetence is always to be preferred as an explanation over malice.[1]

Some public health officials and their defenders dismiss criticism as "hindsight bias." They argue that authorities' mistakes were nevertheless based on the best scientific evidence that was available at the time. Tom Woods has offered a devastating critique of this "hindsight bias" explanation. In *Diary of a Psychosis: How Public Health Disgraced Itself During COVID Mania*,[2] Woods

---

1. Many corporate media sources later *began* to acknowledge the complexities of various COVID questions and reported on the inconsistencies of public health—perhaps too little, too late: Jacob Stern, "The Great Pandemic Hand-Washing Blooper," *The Atlantic*, 24 October 2024 <https://www.the-atlantic.com/health/archive/2022/10/covid-pandemic-airborne-virus-transmission-hand-washing/671831/>; Deborah Netburn, "A timeline of the CDC's advice on face masks," *Los Angeles Times*, 27 July 2021 <https://www.latimes.com/science/story/2021-07-27/timeline-cdc-mask-guidance-during-covid-19-pandemic>; "The Startling Evidence on Learning Loss Is In," *The New York Times* Editorial Board, 18 November 2023 <https://www.nytimes.com/2023/11/18/opinion/pandemic-school-learning-loss.html>; Sarah Sloat, "Menstrual changes after Covid vaccines may be far more common than previously known," *NBC News*, 15 July 2022 <https://www.nbcnews.com/science/science-news/menstruation-changes-covid-vaccines-rcna38348.>: "'[Menstruation] gets ignored because of the structure of science,' Lee, an assistant professor at Tulane University, said. 'There are very few senior people in science and medicine who are not white men. It's just not something they are thinking about as part of their lived experience.'"

2. Thomas E. Woods, Jr., *Diary of a Psychosis: How Public Health Disgraced Itself During COVID Mania* (Libertarian Institute, 2023).

has published the entries from his daily newsletter (only lightly edited) from 23 March 2020 through 1 June 2023 that pertain to the COVID crisis. This might sound at first like a rather uninteresting and useless assemblage. But Woods offers snapshots of the knowledge available and the questions asked "in the moment": information, data, and questions gathered from the news and other sources. The result is in fact a "diary" of the COVID crisis as it unfolded, which is sufficient to demonstrate that *all along the way*: 1) thoughtful people (often without formal scientific training) were asking good questions about the spread of the virus and the effectiveness of countermeasures; 2) countermeasures were demonstrably not working; and 3) public health officials ignored these questions, objections, and the data itself. In the Foreword to *Diary of a Psychosis*, Jay Bhattacharya writes:

> The punchline was clear for anyone with eyes to see. Though political leaders and public health authorities, clothing themselves in the moral authority of The Science™ itself, might claim the credit for the waning of the virus, in fact, the mandates, lockdowns, and other anti-scientific interventions they promulgated and imposed had little or nothing to do with the spread of a highly infectious virus spread by breath.[3]

Even within the "fog of war," there were thoughtful people who were eager for robust scientific debate, and the resources for such a debate. If they had been listened to, things could have been different: there would have been less social and economic damage, less divisiveness and alienation, less physical suffering and loss of life, and public health authorities might have gained trust rather than destroyed it.

---

3. Jay Bhattacharya, "Foreword," in Woods, *Diary of a Psychosis*, x.

Regarding the question of intent, we unfortunately do now have evidence of vast coordination of censorship across health authorities, politicians, governments, corporate media, and social media. This coordination created the illusion of consensus on key issues, and served to manufacture consent among the public for far-reaching government measures to quell the virus.

Censorship

Governments Pressured Technology Companies

Thanks to reporting published in "the Twitter files"[4] (December 2022) and "the Facebook files"[5] (January 2023), and the discovery phases of various lawsuits filed in 2023 and 2024 by individuals and state attorneys general against the US government and certain government officials (including *Berenson v. Biden*, *Murthy v. Missouri*, and *Kennedy et al v. Biden et al*), we now know that US government authorities worked with (even pressured) social media and tech companies to suppress minority viewpoints.

Even though a majority of Americans are not active on social media, Twitter (now X, but I will use the names interchangeably) in particular is a forum where influential members of government, media, and the policy apparatus communicate with one another. Twitter at its best is a "public square" where it is possible for influential public figures to debate topics of public interest, share information, but also to be questioned and commented upon by the public.

---

4. Matt Taibbi, "The Twitter Files," *The Twitter Files* Substack, 12 April 2023 (originally on Twitter 2 December 2022) <https://twitterfiles.substack.com/p/1-thread-the-twitter-files>; David Zweig, "How Twitter Rigged the Covid Debate," *The Free Press*, 26 December 2022 <https://www.thefp.com/p/how-twitter-rigged-the-covid-debate>.

5. Robby Soave, "Inside the Facebook Files: Emails Reveal the CDC's Role in Silencing COVID-19 Dissent," *Reason*, 19 January 2023 <https://reason.com/2023/01/19/facebook-files-emails-cdc-covid-vaccines-censorship/>.

In hindsight, it is almost inevitable that government authorities would seek to control Twitter debates that might undermine public consent for their preferred measures. This pressure from government authorities was revealed in the so-called "Twitter Files" reporting. Bowles's tongue-in-cheek commentary captures the hilarity of the providential events that led to these revelations:

> A conservative humor site called The Babylon Bee that made fun of the [Hunter Biden] laptop situation and various progressive mores of the day? They were locked out of Twitter, lest they tell too many offensive jokes about the daily news, which it was important never to jest about. Then, as you know, a strange thing happened. Elon Musk, annoyed by all of this, bought Twitter. He paid $44 billion for it—which seems like a lot unless you are the richest man in the world. Everyone at the newspapers and all the hardworking censors at the social media companies were upset! How could he buy Twitter? Twitter was meant to be the playground of this set—the place where folks could carefully control and quiet anyone who disagreed with the day's message. It was a crisis. And then Musk did something even stranger: he opened up the company's archives—emails, Slack messages, internal tools—for a group of journalists to pore over, with zero interference. Those journalists were Matt Taibbi, Michael Shellenberger, and the *Free Press* team, including friends such as David Zweig and Abigail Shrier.[6]

---

6. Nellie Bowles, "The Free Press Wins a Prize for Excellence in Investigative Journalism," *The Free Press*, 6 November 2023 <https://www.thefp.com/p/the-free-press-wins-dao-prize>.

"The Twitter Files" refers to reporting done by these journalists, published first on Twitter itself (a condition set by Twitter's new owner Elon Musk), and then in several online venues, mainly the Substack sites of each journalist. These reporters uncovered extensive correspondence between Twitter employees and government officials, including public health officials and members of the intelligence community. Among many other topics, this correspondence revealed government officials pressuring Twitter to censor certain kinds of information regarding COVID (lockdowns, masks, vaccines, treatments), suspend specific users (the so-called "Disinformation Dozen"), and even "shadow-ban" or silently/surreptitiously downgrade certain users (i.e., making their content not sharable, or making it less visible than the algorithms would have without any interference).

Facebook (along with Instagram, owned by Facebook's parent company, Meta) is less influential than Twitter as a public forum. But Facebook and Instagram have many more users than Twitter, and Facebook remains a place where people find one another in groups over common interests. Soave's "Facebook Files" reporting revealed that Facebook routinely censored posts that were critical of lockdowns and COVID vaccines, posts or groups which promoted off-label treatments such as ivermectin and hydroxychloroquine, or which spoke of possible COVID vaccine injuries. This prevented suffering people from finding one another and sharing possible ameliorations and treatments. Regardless of whether one finds all these stories credible (either the attribution of injury to COVID vaccines, or stories of effective treatments), these individuals should have been free to seek help and ideas that might have alleviated their suffering.

Government pressure was applied to other tech companies, as well. YouTube, owned by Google's parent company, still censors such content: removing, demonetizing or downranking videos, with an apparent "moving target" of forbidden topics related to COVID[7]—users will still see informational warnings attached to YouTube videos. Amazon was pressured to remove books skeptical of official claims about COVID vaccines.[8]

These internal communications do reveal that many employees and executives at tech companies were eager to comply with government requests to censor, because they agreed ideologically with the direction of the censorship. But even those who were hesitant or even opposed to censoring speech on their platforms had little choice—if they did not comply, the government could threaten their business with various kinds of legal action that would, at the very least, be quite costly.[9]

Backdoors to Censorship: NGOs

These journalistic exposés have revealed that government officials and agents pressured technology companies through direct contact. Even though it is illegal in the US for the government to censor political speech, this was an attempt to circumvent the First Amendment: induce or pressure tech companies to "voluntarily" censor their users (typically the terms of service allow companies to restrict speech on their platforms). This certainly violates the spirit of the First Amendment, however.

---

7. Brianna Herlihy, "Sen. Johnson demands YouTube answer for 'repeated censorship' on COVID, conservative viewpoints," *Fox News*, 22 September 2022 <https://www.foxnews.com/politics/sen-johnson-demands-youtube-answer-repeated-censorship-covid-conservative-viewpoints>.

8. David Zimmerman, "Biden White House Pressured Amazon to Censor Vaccine-Skeptical Books, Internal Emails Reveal," *National Review*, 6 February 2024 <https://www.nationalreview.com/news/biden-white-house-pressured-amazon-to-censor-vaccine-skeptical-books-internal-emails-reveal/>; Jacob Sullum, "Was Amazon 'Free to Ignore' White House Demands That It Suppress Anti-Vaccine Books?" *Reason*, 7 February 2024 <https://reason.com/2024/02/07/was-amazon-free-to-ignore-white-house-demands-that-it-suppress-anti-vaccine-books/>.

9. It is not at all unlike the *mafia* "representative" who shows up at the restaurant, and says to the owner, "Nice restaurant you got here—shame if something was to happen to it!" The threat is implied, but obvious.

Another form of online censorship is emerging. Several media outlets have all recently reported the following pattern. Western governments face constitutional hurdles to suppressing dissident political speech. In order to circumvent this limitation, government agencies or their direct military contractors create non-governmental organizations (NGOs[10]), research institutes/think tanks, and other ostensibly "public interest" non-profits. These NGOs then in turn create policy papers, lists of topics of so-called "misinformation, disinformation and malinformation," and lists of individuals and news sources that ought not to be trusted.[11] Tech and social media companies then use these "privately-generated" lists of topics, individuals and sources to self-censor on their platforms. Companies that sell advertising also use these lists to starve "undesirable" websites of ad revenue—corporations who advertise want assurances that their ads will not appear alongside "objectionable" content, and so they consent. *UnHerd*, whose journalism leans contrarian but publishes a wide range of views, discovered this when they ran afoul of something called the "Global Disinformation Index" because they had published gender-critical feminist Kathleen Stock.[12] *Public* and *Racket News* reported that another organization, the Cyber Threat Intelligence League (CTIL), appears to have been founded by "data scientists and defense and intelligence veterans but whose tactics over time appear

---

10. Some are more appropriately described as 'GONGOs': government-organized non-governmental organizations.

11. "Malinformation" is defined by the US Department of Homeland Security as: "genuine information, typically private or revealing, that may be distributed in a campaign to cause harm to a person's reputation in furtherance of the campaign's objective." Put differently, "malinformation" is information that is factually true but may undermine a government objective or authority. See Matthew Harwood, "Government Attempts to Label Speech Misinformation, Disinformation, and Malinformation Are a Free-Speech Nightmare," *Foundation for Individual Rights and Expression*, 21 November 2022 <https://www.thefire.org/news/government-attempts-label-speech-misinformation-disinformation-and-malinformation-are-free>.

12. Freddie Sayers, "Inside the disinformation industry: A government-sponsored agency is censoring journalism," *UnHerd*, 17 April 2024 <https://unherd.com/2024/04/inside-the-disinformation-industry/>.

to have been absorbed into multiple official projects, including those of the Department of Homeland Security (DHS)." The CTIL crafted broad plans for internet censorship, that eventually led to the seeming integration of the Western intelligence agencies with the social media companies. This reporting corroborates earlier work by *The Intercept* about the US Department of Homeland Security's new powers granted in 2018 when the Cybersecurity and Infrastructure Security Agency Act (CISA Act) was passed.[13]

Even though this type of censorship is not directly government restriction of speech, it nevertheless represents a troubling attitude toward speech and public debate, which presumes that "those who possess authority" know better, and will use soft pressure backed by real threats—a velvet glove concealing a hard fist—to punish dissent, allegedly for the public good.

The Result: Fake Consensus, Manufactured Consent

No doubt, some of my readers will find these assertions difficult to believe. I would strongly encourage those who are skeptical to read the reporting I have cited here, presented by credible sources on publicly-available information. It is also important to note that these efforts at censorship preceded the COVID crisis, and continue to evolve even after COVID is past.

I have argued that both ineptitude and intentional censorship of debate resulted in authorities' poor results during COVID. In this framework, malicious intent is not necessary to explain the devastating results. All that is required is a convergence of benevolently paternalistic beliefs (i.e., groupthink) on the part of elites,

---

13. Ken Klippenstein and Lee Fang, "Truth Cops: Leaked Documents Outline DHS's Plans to Police Disinformation," *The Intercept,* 31 October 2022 <https://theintercept.com/2022/10/31/social-media-disinformation-dhs/>; Jacob Siegel, "A Guide to Understanding the Hoax of the Century: Thirteen Ways of Looking at Disinformation," *Tablet,* 28 March 2023 <https://www.tabletmag.com/sections/news/articles/guide-understanding-hoax-century-thirteen-ways-looking-disinformation>.

and an unhealthy interaction and interdependence between academia, corporate media, tech companies, and government.[14] We will explore this through the lens of "public choice" in Chapter 16 of this book.

Scholars of propaganda and persuasion have long understood the effectiveness of convincing individuals of the scariness of believing something that no one else believes, and conversely, the apparent satisfaction and safety of being part of a group with common beliefs—Ellul's "lonely crowd,"[15] or Desmet's "mass formation."[16] In an age of digital communication technology and the fragmentation of news dissemination, the ability of authorities to control the range of public discussion on crucial issues was weakened, and power has shifted from hierarchies to networks, as Gurri argues in *The Revolt of the Public*.[17]

It is therefore predictable that elites would seek to move beyond mere persuasion and mass media, and to control or censor those alternative networks of discussion and authority. The fact that the COVID crisis centered on a virus spread by human interaction, and the resulting perception that staying away from another person was the healthy and moral response,[18] led to further isolation of individuals in their homes—this, amidst a "loneliness

14. Expounded notably in the context of US foreign policy by Edward S. Herman and Noam Chomsky, in *Manufacturing Consent: The Political Economy of the Mass Media*, 2nd revised edition (New York: Pantheon Books, 2002 [1988]). In the context of the COVID crisis, see, *inter alia*, Rav Arora, "The Federal Government Paid Media Outlets To Promote The Covid Vaccine," *The Illusion of Consensus* Substack, 28 November 2023 <https://www.illusionconsensus.com/p/the-federal-government-paid-media>.

15. Jacques Ellul, *Propaganda: The Formation of Men's Attitudes*, translated by Konrad Kellen and Jean Lerner (New York: Vintage Books, 1973 [1965]), 147–148.

16. Mattias Desmet, *The Psychology of Totalitarianism*, translated by Els VanBrabant (White River Junction, VT: Chelsea Green Publishing, 2022).

17. Martin Gurri, *The Revolt of the Public and the Crisis of Authority in the New Millennium*, 2nd edition (San Francisco: Stripe Press, 2018 [2014]).

18. I discuss the moralization of sickness in Chapter 14 as an aspect of the social and spiritual damage of the COVID response.

epidemic" pronounced by many Western health authorities in our already highly technologized age.[19] It was a perfect storm.

Censorship and the Church

How did censorship affect churches and Christian communities? As Christian leaders were trying in good faith, amidst the "fog of war," to make decisions about gatherings for worship and discipleship for the good of the flocks under their care, the environment of censorship created an "illusion of consensus" on the key issues relevant to the church that are outlined in Chapter 12. It was therefore difficult for medical professionals and Christian leaders to see critiques of official positions that were offered by other experts (and by concerned, thoughtful citizens who were following the issues closely).

Some Christian leaders who have read this far will object that it is important for someone to be monitoring online speech, and that some speech should be censored for the public good. To those pragmatic readers I would say: simply look at the consequences of the censorship, outlined in the previous chapter.

Consider the implications of this widespread censorship that began to come to light after nearly three years of pandemic guidance promoted online in "mainstream" forums (early 2020 through December 2022 when the Twitter Files were published). How might you as a pastor or lay leader have handled contentious matters differently in your congregation or small group during COVID, if you knew that other experts disagreed with the perspectives to which the authorities were demanding adherence? What if 80% of credentialed experts agreed with the CDC, but 20% disagreed? What is the threshold at which you might have done things differently, or at least insisted to your congregation

---

19. On the importance of community for discipleship and human well-being, see Chapter 7.

that individuals must be free to make their own decisions? Would your church have been as polarized? Would people at the extreme ends of controversial issues have been as numerous or as vociferous? Instead of leading to peace and consensus, censorship only exacerbated tensions.

In retrospect, as Christian leaders we must denounce this censorship as immoral—interfering with the free speech of scientists, doctors, and members of the public. Even if the government-enforced perspectives had turned out to be correct (which I have already contested), minority positions should still be permitted to exist (and cross-examined with logic and evidence). Furthermore, such censorship was irresponsible and harmed the public, including members of our congregations, by short-circuiting legitimate scientific debate.[20]

As it turns out, on many of the issues outlined, the minority perspective is now acknowledged by mainstream/corporate sources to be correct or at least within the realm of legitimate debate—but the damage to the public and to political discourse has already been done.

---

20. Scott W. Atlas, "America's COVID Response Was Based on Lies," *Newsweek* Opinion 6 March 2023 <https://www.newsweek.com/america-covid-response-was-based-lies-opinion-1785177>.

CHAPTER 14 | The Damage of the COVID Response

The Social Damage of the COVID Response

Numerous authors and research groups have begun to tabulate and chronicle the damage of the response to COVID, across all dimensions and domains of society.[1] No doubt, this task will occupy many historians and social scientists for decades to come, and the "just allotment of memory"[2] will be hotly contested.

It is not possible or necessary for me to replicate this research, but a reminder of the different sorts of costs to individuals and societies is important before we move on to considering the damage to the church and its gospel witness.

First of all, we must remember the lives of those who died because of COVID (and the families who grieve them), and those who became seriously ill and live with lasting health effects. If

---

1. A website, collateralglobal.org, has the following mission: "researching, understanding, and communicating the effectiveness and collateral impacts of the Mandated Non-Pharmaceutical Interventions (MNPIs) taken by governments worldwide in response to the COVID-19 pandemic" (<https://collateralglobal.org/about>). The growing literature in this area includes: Toby Green and Thomas Fazi, *The Covid Consensus: The Global Assault on Democracy and the Poor? A Critique from the Left*, 2nd edition (Hurst, 2023); Gigi Foster, Paul Frijters, Michael Baker, *The Great Covid Panic: What Happened, Why, and What to Do Next* (Austin, TX: Brownstone Institute, 2021); Thomas E. Woods, Jr., *Diary of a Psychosis: How Public Health Disgraced Itself During COVID Mania* (Libertarian Institute, 2023); Thomas E. Woods, Jr., *Collateral Damage: Victims of the Lockdown Regime Tell Their Stories* (2023); Alex Berenson, *Pandemia: How Coronavirus Hysteria Took Over Our Government, Rights, and Lives* (Regnery, 2021).

2. Borrowing the phrase from Paul Ricoeur, *Memory, History, Forgetting*, trans. Kathleen Blamey and David Pellauer (Chicago: University of Chicago Press, 2004).

SARS-COV-2 was in some way the product of human reckless-ness or malevolence, those responsible at all levels of government and research should be held accountable.

Regarding the responses to COVID, we must also remember the damage done to:

- The poor and working class in Western countries[3]

- The extreme poor in poor countries/economies, millions of whom were thrown deeper into poverty, prostitution, slavery, and/or starvation by restrictive policies[4]

- Children who were deprived of education and socialization[5]

- Babies and young children who were deprived of nurture, face-to-face interactions, and physical touch

- The elderly and infirm in assisted-living facilities, who were deprived of social connection due to limits on visitation, some in their final months of earthly life.[6] This was es-

---

3. James Allan offers a review of Toby Green and Thomas Fazi, *The Covid Consensus: The Global Assault on Democracy and the Poor? A Critique from the Left*, 2nd edition (Hurst, 2023); Allan, "A Look Back at Lockdowns," *Law & Liberty*, 30 March 2023 <https://lawliberty.org/book-re-view/a-look-back-at-lockdowns/>. "Did lockdowns save lives? Actually, if you focus solely on Covid deaths, even that is not clear. Once you factor in all the other ways people can die—from missed cancer checks, obesity, mental health problems leading to suicides and alcoholism, missed opera-tions, the list goes on and on—it's not even close. Lockdowns led to loads more overall deaths. Just go and check out that Swedish excess data again and watch how bad it gets over the coming years."

4. Jonathan T. Rothwell, Alexandru Cojocaru, Rajesh Srinivasan and Yeon Soo Kim, "Global ev-idence on the economic effects of disease suppression during COVID-19," *Humanities & Social Sciences Communications* (2024) 11:78, <https://doi.org/10.1057/s41599-023-02571-4>.

5. Peter Coy, "Lockdowns Protected Older People. But at What Cost to the Health of Young Adults?" *The New York Times* opinion, 10 June 2022 <https://www.nytimes.com/2022/06/10/opinion/covid-death-young-old.html>; Angie Schmitt, "The Painful Aftermath of School Closures: How did we get it so wrong? What are we gonna do now?," *Unpopular Opinions* Substack, 9 January 2024 <https://angieschmitt.substack.com/p/the-painful-aftermath-of-school-closures>.

6. Anyone who can read this story without becoming outraged has no human feeling: "'Hand of God': Brazilian Nurses Use Gloves Filled with Warm Water to Create 'Human Touch' for Covid-19 Patients," *News18.com*, 10 April 2021 <https://www.news18.com/news/buzz/hand-of-god-brazilian-nurses-use-gloves-filled-with-hot-water-to-create-human-touch-for-covid-19-patients-3622187.html>.

pecially destructive (and likely terrifying) for those with cognitive impairments (Alzheimers, dementia) for whom familiar faces are crucial for their well-being

- Those who are deaf or hearing-impaired (many who are elderly) who were unable to read their caregivers' or visitors' lips due to mask requirements. For those who are both hearing-impaired *and* have cognitive or memory defects, being unable to understand what caregivers are doing to/ for them can be terrifying.

- Victims of abuse (especially women and children) who were trapped in homes with their abusers with no one to notice marks of abuse

- Those who suffer from depression, anxiety and mental illness

- Those who were driven to suicide by isolation and loss of work and experiences that made their lives meaningful; and their families and friends who mourn them

- Those who struggle with addictions who are/were in need of ongoing support

- Those who were unable to say goodbye and/or reconcile with dying loved ones due to quarantine requirements

- Those who missed treatments/screenings for other illnesses, and will suffer more and/or die sooner as a result (and the families who will mourn them)

- Those who were injured by vaccines

- Those who were denied the right to try approved drugs off-label

- Those who had family relationships or friendships torn apart by seemingly irreconcilable differences[7]

- Those who were compelled to take a vaccine against their will, or by having their jobs, scholarships or other livelihoods threatened. For many individuals, the choice to get a vaccine was technically voluntary in a legal sense, but was not *euvoluntary* or *truly voluntary* (more on this distinction in Chapter 16).

- Those who lost their jobs or had significant restrictions of freedom for declining a vaccine

- Those who were deprived of freedom due to vaccine passport regimes. This includes those who were unable to travel, work or conduct commerce due to declining a vaccine, *and* those who complied but were nevertheless subject to intrusive and inconvenient checks such as scanning/checking vaccine certificates upon entering a store.[8]

- Those who were denied other medical treatment because they declined a COVID vaccine

The Spiritual Damage of the COVID Response

The preceding list of the categories of harms to society by lockdowns, mandates, and segregation, provides context and a point

---

7. Mark Oshinskie, "On Broken Friendships," *Brownstone Institute*, 24 October 2023 <https://brownstone.org/articles/on-broken-friendships/>.

8. Many progressives and libertarians are rightly concerned about disparate impacts of policing and potentially dangerous encounters with police, especially for racial minorities. A system that requires checkpoints and enforcement officers increases the potential for dangerous confrontations (for officers and for citizens).

of departure for describing the sorts of damage that have been done in many Christian communities.[9]

Cancelling or Compromising Corporate Worship

Some churches were entirely closed for in-person worship for many months, even nearly a year.[10] This really cannot be considered excusable beyond a few initial weeks in March–May of 2020. If corporate worship is an essential spiritual sustenance for Christians and a proclamation of the gospel for unbelievers, then suspending corporate worship for extended periods of time constitutes a failure of shepherding and mission.

Various congregations were compelled or chose to compromise their worship in ways that undermined the effectiveness of the means of grace (see Chapter 6). As I described above, some mitigation efforts were not pleasant, but did not fundamentally change the structure of worship (distancing, hand washing, masks)—tradeoffs were made for the sake of fellowship. But other churches suspended or changed their eucharistic practice, which in some high-church traditions is very significant. Some churches submitted to a ban on singing[11] or fellowship times.

Online meetings with church members are demonstrably not as satisfying and beneficial as in-person worship. Thus, those who relied upon so-called "online church" have suffered, or have even stopped participating due to its lack of power (see Chapter 3). In terms of a "silver lining," there is no good evidence that the

9. Dean Broyles, "Lockdowns Had a Devastating Impact on Religion," *Brownstone Institute*, 1 April 2022 <https://brownstone.org/articles/lockdowns-had-a-devastating-impact-on-religion/>.

10. Christine Black, "The Speakeasy Churches of 2020," *Brownstone Institute*, 15 July 2022 <https://brownstone.org/articles/the-speakeasy-churches-of-2020/>; Auguste Meyrat, "Covid and the Gates of Hell: The Church won't survive another Covid scare," *The American Conservative*, 16 September 2023 <https://www.theamericanconservative.com/covid-and-the-gates-of-hell/>.

11. Pat Ashworth, "Ban on choral singing based on flawed evidence, study suggests," *Church Times*, 16 November 2022 <https://www.churchtimes.co.uk/articles/2022/18-november/news/uk/ban-on-choral-singing-based-on-flawed-evidence-study-suggests>.

widespread practice of livestreaming of church services has expanded the reach of the gospel, beyond what was possible already through online gospel/teaching videos created for those purposes. On the contrary, online streaming gave Christians who already went to church a window into other churches and (perhaps) more reasons to be dissatisfied with their own local church.[12]

In my initial statement in Chapter 10 concerning "grave errors," I distinguished between *opening churches* so that congregants could make their own choices, and binding people's consciences to say that faithful Christians *must attend* every worship service regardless of their risk profile—the latter is an improper exercise of spiritual authority, which will be further explored below. From the perspective of the congregant, many individuals were willing to risk contracting COVID in order to benefit from attending church. In Chapter 8, I argued that in-person worship and discipleship is especially crucial for younger people, who have less experience with the discipline necessary to engage in individual devotional activities—and that this fact is often lost on church leaders, who tend to be older. Even if older (and otherwise at-risk) leaders and congregants thought it prudent to avoid gatherings, they could have encouraged younger leaders and members of the congregation to gather (I know several older leaders who took this approach).

The result of widespread church closure is that church attendance has dropped since COVID, especially among children,

---

12. This is yet another negative consequence of the "exposure to the best" phenomenon, to go along with those described in Chapters 6 and 8.

Living abroad and engaging a local church in a non-native language is challenging. I can attest to the letdown after the tantalizing online "reunion" that many cross-cultural workers temporarily enjoyed with their home churches and supporting churches back in their countries of origin in early 2020. These online "reunions" served to remind us of the satisfying fellowships we had left behind in order to serve cross-culturally, and, by comparison, of all that was difficult about engaging our church in the country of service.

young adults, and those who were "on the fence"/marginal about Christian faith and church involvement.[13] Unfortunately, in response to COVID measures, many Christians adopted the view that church participation is not essential for the life of a Christian disciple. According to LifeWay research, the number of American evangelicals who agreed with the statement, "Worshiping alone or with one's family is a valid replacement for regularly attending church," rose from 39% in 2020 to 54% in 2022.[14] *Christianity Today* reported in April 2022: "26 Million Americans Stopped Reading the Bible Regularly During COVID-19."[15]

Fear and social and governmental pressure to undertake mitigation efforts or close church altogether caused great divisions in Christian communities,[16] not just in churches, but in Christian colleges and universities (my own experience—see later in this chapter).

It is not hyperbole to assert that a number of people (only God knows how many) *died spiritually* due to the closure of in-person church worship and fellowship for extended periods during the pandemic. For Christians who claim to value the salvation of souls and should not "fear those who destroy only the body" (Matt 10:28), and who believe in bodily resurrection, these

---

13. Roger E. Olson, "What the COVID Pandemic Means for Churches," *Patheos* blog, 16 July 2022 <https://www.patheos.com/blogs/rogereolson/2022/07/what-the-covid-pandemic-means-for-churches/>.

14. Aaron Earls, "Americans' Theological Beliefs Changed to Suit Post-Pandemic Practice," *Lifeway Research*, 19 September 2022 <https://research.lifeway.com/2022/09/19/americans-theological-beliefs-changed-to-suit-post-pandemic-practice/?ecid=PDM260974&bid=1173958734>.

15. Adam MacInnis, "Report: 26 Million Americans Stopped Reading the Bible Regularly During COVID-19," *Christianity Today*, 20 April 2022 <https://www.christianitytoday.com/news/2022/april/state-of-bible-reading-decline-report-26-million.html>.

16. Steve Templeton, "How Covid Panic Destroyed Communities: Our Church and My Story," *Brownstone Institute*, 3 December 2021 <https://brownstone.org/articles/how-covid-panic-destroyed-communities-our-church-and-my-story/>.

spiritual deaths should weigh most heavily on us when the toll of
the pandemic response is tallied.[17]

Moralization of Sickness ("...Wash Your Hands, You Sinners..." [James 4:8])

As a Christian leader, it is my special duty to draw attention to
the moralizing language that surrounded COVID, especially in
the first year or so. There was an assumption, explicitly or implicitly, that those who had been infected had become so because
of their own reckless behavior or by the recklessness of others.
The language of "love for neighbor," "protecting the vulnerable,"
and "sacrifice" had become so associated with measures to (supposedly) prevent the spread of COVID, that it allowed then for
moral condemnation of those who did not take those same measures, or who contracted COVID (as we all eventually did).

I myself recall the shame I felt when having to call a friend in
November 2020 to tell her that our family had tested positive for
COVID just a few days after she had visited our home and taken
her mask off for only fifteen minutes in our presence. My embar-
rassment was what (I imagine) a person feels when having to call

---

17. On a related subject, during the height of the pandemic Edwards, following C.S. Lewis's
"Learning in War-Time," made a strident, positive case for continuing theological education in
some form amidst the crisis. If academic theology is superfluous, then perhaps we should not
bother with it even in "normal times"—but if it is "singable theology," i.e., theology that leads
to worship, then it must continue *especially* in times of crisis: "Wherever theological education is
deemed not to matter 'during wartime', this only shows how little the theologians, educators and
leaders have made theology heard in showing the Church her perennial need for it and in singing it
well. Whatever the time happens to be, we must insist upon theological education. Whatever crisis
happens to be raging, the Church must be reminded that she is always in war-time and always
has been (cf. Eph 6:12). Pursuing theological education might well be seen as an irresponsible
ruse to avoid our peculiar battlefield, but to those truly committed to think, pray, read, speak and
sing well of God within it, theology might just be the most responsible thing a person *could* do."
Aaron Edwards, "The Perennial Urgency of Theological Education," *EJT* 30.1 (2021): 167–190
[188–189] <https://doi.org/10.5117/EJT2021.1.009.EDWA>.

a sexual partner to confess a positive STI test. I had internalized the moralization of the spread of disease.[18]

Some public health officials were alarmed by this moralization and tried to draw attention to the dangers of thinking of infectious disease in this way. There are numerous historical precedents of societies blaming outbreaks on the dangerous "others" in their midst: witches, Jewish communities, Roma people, etc. Some drew parallels to the unfruitfulness of such language surrounding the spread of HIV/AIDS. In the West, HIV/AIDS was mainly a disease of drug abusers or the sexually promiscuous (usually men who have sex with men), but this obscured the fact that many people contract HIV/AIDS through entirely innocent means: blood transfusion, accidental needle stick, or intercourse with an unfaithful spouse.[19] Moreover, the moral condemnation heaped upon HIV/AIDS sufferers makes it difficult for such people to seek testing and treatment which could save their lives and mitigate the spread of disease—moralizing harms public health efforts.[20]

Christians can look to the biblical examples of Job's friends who attributed his suffering to some specific moral failing; or to the disciples who asked Jesus, "Rabbi, who sinned, this man or his parents, that he would be born blind?" (John 9:2)[21] For COVID, a respiratory disease spread by completely innocent and inevitable (even necessary!) human interaction (through breathing, i.e., aerosolized virus), moralization served no purpose other than to

---

18. Our friend did not test positive for COVID following that visit. She did eventually contract COVID at least once—after receiving the primary series of the COVID vaccine. We remain friends to this day.

19. Also, many people who commit such sins (promiscuous sex, drug use) *do not* get HIV/AIDS. If HIV/AIDS is the just punishment for such sins, then God is unjust.

20. Drs. Drew Pinsky, Vinay Prasad, and Monica Gandhi spoke extensively about these troubling parallels/contrasts between public health messaging during the HIV/AIDS epidemic and the COVID pandemic.

21. Also, Luke 13:1–5, in which Jesus addresses the issue of tragedy apart from direct human moral responsibility.

incite fear, division, and anger.[22] This alternate (unbiblical) moral structure of *healthy* = *good/loving, sick* = *reckless/prideful* should have been denounced by Christian leaders seeking to shape our public discourse by the norm of scripture. Instead, as we will see below, many Christian leaders accepted this alternate morality, causing tremendous division and spiritual damage.

Oversimplifying "Neighbor-Love"

Another mistake made by Christian leaders was to accept the simplistic definition of "neighbor love" that was given to them by outside authorities.[23] Especially with respect to lockdowns and vaccines, one side seized the moral high ground by defining "neighbor love" as abiding by lockdown/separation orders, encouraging universal masking, and then later, getting the vaccine.[24] The fact that there are significant downsides to separating from people we love and serve, and the fact that the vaccine did not stop transmission of the virus (see Chapter 12), mean that "neighbor love" could not be simply defined as adherence to these dicta. And yet, once the "loving" path was defined in one

---

22. Thomas Harrington, "The Full Secularization of the Doctrine of Original Sin," *Brownstone Institute*, 6 December 2021 <https://brownstone.org/articles/the-full-secularization-of-the-doctrine-of-original-sin/>; James Wood, "The COVID Regime as Stoicheic Order," *Theopolis*, 21 September 2021 <https://theopolisinstitute.com/the-covid-regime-as-stoicheic-order/>.

23. This is not unlike what some Christians do with the term "justice" or "social justice": importing unbiblical or non-Christian definitions of justice into interpretation of biblical texts concerning "justice."

24. Andrew Wong, "Stop using religion to fight COVID-19 vaccine. Taking it is the Christian thing to do," *USA Today* opinion, 28 July 2021 <https://www.usatoday.com/story/opinion/voices/2021/07/28/take-covid-19-vaccine-its-christian-thing-do/5389873001/>; "Should Pastors Speak Up About the COVID-19 Vaccine? With Christians split on the issue, some urge vaccination as a form of neighborly love, while others leave it up to conscience," compiled by Rebecca Randall, *Christianity Today*, 11 December 2020 <https://www.christianitytoday.com/ct/2020/december-web-only/should-pastors-speak-up-about-covid-19-vaccine.html>.
    Andrew T. Walker has commendably repented of his earlier contention that Christians should take the vaccine based on "love of neighbor": "The Wax Nose of Neighbor Love," *Public Discourse*, 15 April 2024 <https://www.thepublicdiscourse.com/2024/04/93212/>.

direction from the beginning, it was nearly impossible to discuss, nuance, debate or contradict.[25]

Binding Consciences

By taking a public stand on debatable issues, some Christian leaders bound their followers' consciences[26] on issues that were in fact debatable and nuanced. The loudest pastoral voices claimed that church closures, and later, vaccines, were a moral imperative.[27] Others declared that Christians who skipped church were living in fear not in faith, and later, that vaccines were utterly immoral, representing a lack of trust in God. Both of these manipulations from opposite extreme positions fail to respect the *imago Dei* in each person, who should be free to make decisions on what goes into his/her own body, or what sorts of risks of transmission were worth the trade-off of being with other people. (The rationale of "negative externalities" does not apply because vaccines and lockdown orders did not halt the spread of the virus.)

However, the leadership voices improperly binding consciences *against* vaccines were drowned out by the voices using spiritual manipulation to compel hesitant believers to *take* a vaccine—voices that were in some cases funded by state actors

---

25. Michael J. Sutton, "Covid Theology in the Australian Church," *Brownstone Institute*, 3 February 2023 <https://brownstone.org/articles/covid-theology-in-the-australian-church/>.

26. "Binding the conscience" is a term used in several of the Protestant confessions. It refers to a church authority (a council or a teaching) pronouncing as a biblical obligation a belief or a practice upon which scripture has not directly spoken. Key biblical texts protect the believer's conscience on debatable matters: Gal 3:1; 1 Cor 8; Rom 14. Binding the conscience is a form of legalism, because it adds "law" to the true gospel. See Brad Littlejohn, "Binding Consciences: Why We Do It, How We Do It, and Why It's So Dangerous," *9Marks.com*, 29 September 2020 <https://www.9marks.org/article/binding-consciences-why-we-do-it-how-we-do-it-and-why-its-so-dangerous/>.

27. Phillip Jensen, "Getting Vaccinated is Our Christian Duty," personal blog, 29 July 2021 <https://phillipjensen.com/resources/getting-vaccinated-is-our-christian-duty/>; Neil Chambers, "Thank God and Roll Up Your Sleeve," *TGC Australia Edition*, 3 May 2021 <https://au.thegospelcoalition.org/article/thanks-god-and-roll-up-your-sleeve/>.

(explored further in Chapter 15) and protected by state-compelled censorship.

A particularly grievous example of such manipulation is an article published in October 2021 by respected pastor, author and scholar John Piper, entitled, "A Reason to be Vaccinated: Freedom."[28] Piper purports to be arguing for "radical medical freedom," that the Christian's conscience should not be bound either to take a vaccine or to reject a vaccine. But Piper makes clear from the outset, and throughout the article, that his aim is to convince a Christian reader to "freely" receive a COVID vaccine, for the good of society. He lists frightening statistics regarding the dangers of hospitalization and death, linking to mainstream news sources from the time. He does not want Christians who are on the fence and have no other conscience objections, to avoid vaccination due to political pressure: "You are free to say with integrity, 'My decision to be vaccinated is not a political decision. It is not right wing, or left wing. It is a biblically informed act of love.'" Here Piper adopts the spurious basis for vaccination, namely that it supposedly prevents the spread.

To say that Piper's article constitutes an evenhanded defense of medical freedom against compulsion from both sides, reflects a (perhaps willful) misunderstanding of the asymmetry of the social pressure that individual Christians were facing regarding vaccination.[29] While there were a handful of fringe voices improperly arguing that it would be immoral for Christians to receive any of the COVID vaccines, there were *far more* voices (within the

---

28. John Piper, "A Reason to Be Vaccinated: Freedom," *Desiring God*, 19 October 2021 <https://www.desiringgod.org/articles/a-reason-to-be-vaccinated-freedom>.

29. See also the disappointing conclusions of Stenschke, who also gives the impression that the legal situation in his country (Germany) was neutral with respect to vaccination (it was not—the so-called '3G' system) and that opposing pressures within churches requiring or forbidding vaccinations were equal (they were not): Christoph Stenschke, "The 'Strong' and the 'Weak' in Romans 14:1–15:13 and Covid-19-Related Tensions in Christian Congregations: The Prospects and Perils of Relating Current Concerns to Sacred Scripture," *Neotestamentica* 57.1 (2023): 25–56 [41–44].

church, and without) using manipulation, compulsion or force to compel vaccine-hesitant people to take them. Churches were not expelling people for receiving vaccines. Christians were not threatened with losing their jobs, businesses or scholarships if they received the vaccines. Every compelling force in church and society was marshaled to bind consciences and compel behavior in the direction of vaccination.

A principled defense of medical freedom from Pastor John without a foot on one side of the scale would have been a breath of fresh air, but sadly this was not what we received from him. Instead, Piper offered a nod to the principle of conscience while passive-aggressively nudging his readers toward the "correct" choice: vaccination.[30]

The Spiritual Harm of Segregation

Some Christian communities chose to require vaccination as a condition of worshipping in-person (and some chose to comply with requirements from secular authorities rather than engage in civil disobedience).[31] Other churches relegated unvaccinated

---

30. Some particularly egregious examples: "If the shoe fits, put it on, check your conscience, consult your doctor, and go get vaccinated. If it doesn't, go tearfully and cheerfully on your way. Tearfully, because over 4.5 million people have died from COVID-19 worldwide (including over 700,000 Americans). And cheerfully, because Christ makes it miraculously possible to love people by being 'sorrowful yet always rejoicing' (2 Corinthians 6:10)."

"Christians are owned by no man—no society, no company, no clan, no family, no school, no military, no government, no political interest group. God alone owns us. And God alone rules us. We are not ruled by any man. We are free from all human ownership and rule. When we submit, we do so for the Lord's sake. Because he said to. God's ownership of his people strips every decisive entitlement from human authority. It turns every act of human compliance into worship. When we submit, we do so for the glory of our one Owner and Master." Piper, "A Reason to Be Vaccinated: Freedom."

31. Peter Mullen, "O Come All Ye Vaccinated," *The Conservative Woman*, 23 November 2021 <https://www.conservativewoman.co.uk/o-come-all-ye-vaccinated/>; R.R. Reno, "Vaccine Passports for Churches?" *First Things*, 3 September 2021 <https://www.firstthings.com/web-exclusives/2021/09/vaccine-passports-for-churches>.

individuals to a separate worship space.[32] It is important to understand why this is wrong and did such spiritual harm to the church, and why some remain alienated from the church due to lack of repentance by leadership.

In Galatians 2, Paul describes how some people (not the leaders) had snuck in, to "spy out our liberty which we have in Christ Jesus, in order to bring us into bondage" (Gal 2:4). Thus, leaders need to keep watch to ensure that our people are not slipped back into bondage of adding some requirement to the gospel.

Instead, however, Peter had withdrawn from the Gentiles because of fear (2:11–14). One could almost imagine Peter or James making the case that table-separation (fellowship, and the Eucharist) of Jews and Gentiles at their gatherings was necessary to maintain church unity. But what they failed to grasp is that the fellowship of Jews and Gentiles was not just a matter of getting along from across the room. It was a necessary testimony of the work of the cross in reconciling peoples to one another across boundaries of difference as individuals are reconciled to God through faith in Christ (Gal 3:26–29). Paul describes this as a "testimony" to the fallen spiritual powers that had held Gentile individuals and peoples in bondage (Eph 3:10), but who are now "disarmed" (Col 2:15). This is why amoral[33] differences (*adiaphora*) must not be allowed to divide the body of Christ (Col 2:16). God

---

32. "Redeemer Presbyterian Church in New York City, which was founded by Tim Keller and pastored by him until his retirement in 2017, has instituted a vaccination requirement for those wanting to sit on the first floor of the auditorium at its downtown campus during Sunday morning worship services. …According to the downtown church's website, 'Individuals who are fully vaccinated (two weeks have elapsed since your final dose or single-shot dose) will be allowed to sit on the first floor of the auditorium without social distancing and masks will be optional.'" Dale Chamberlain, "Redeemer Presbyterian Church in NYC Requiring Vaccinations to Sit on First Floor of Auditorium," *ChurchLeaders.com*, 26 October 2021 <https://churchleaders.com/news/408495-redeemer-presbyterian-vaccination.html>.

33. I am not referring to people who are under church discipline and thereby excluded on grounds of moral behavior. For the sake of the testimony of the church and the spiritual good of the individual, such people should be "put out of the church" until they repent (1 Cor 5; 2 Cor 2:1–11).

is especially glorified when people come together to worship him across boundaries of difference (e.g., Rom 15:5–13).[34]

Paul recognized that Peter and James had committed harm to the Gentile believers in Jesus. Peter and James themselves may not have said explicitly to the Gentiles, "You must become circumcised and keep the food laws in order to be believers in Jesus." Peter himself was Jewish and could have eaten at either the Gentile table or the Jewish table withing giving offense. But by allowing the so-called "circumcision party" (the Jewish adherents who believed Gentiles needed to keep the ceremonial law in order to follow Jesus) to separate themselves on the basis of *adiaphora* (amoral matters of conscience or preference), the Apostles had compromised the integrity of the body and robbed the Gentile

---

34. A similar concern is found in Romans 14:1–15:13, where concerns about eating idol-meat threatened to divide the table fellowship of the church. The lesson of Paul on this occasion is not: make any concessions to the ill-founded taboos or paranoias of any members—but rather: table fellowship trumps *adiaphora*, because God is glorified in the unity of the church.

In a notable but disappointing attempt to apply scripture to the COVID-19 situation in churches, Stenschke assesses the tensions in Christian communities about whether and how to meet for worship and fellowship as follows: "…In view of the differences between then and now, direct 'application' of Romans 14–15 to the polarisations within Christian congregations during the Covid-19 pandemic would be highly problematic. Back then, the contentious issues 'only' concerned matters of food, drink, and days. Different positions and practices would affect individuals in different ways (Paul took the issues seriously enough to address them in some detail), but these differences did *not* have the potential to immediately affect their health: none of the positions that appear in Romans 14–15 is potentially life-threatening or physically dangerous to those who hold or disregard them. When it comes to the measures taken at the height of the current pandemic, the situation is different. Through a lack of consideration and their refusal to be vaccinated, people not only became ill and expected others to help them under such circumstances (perhaps risking their own health in doing so) but could also transfer the virus to those around them and could, depending on the course of the disease, cause massive damage to those to whom they spread the disease. When it comes to issues of nutrition and festive days, it is relatively easy, at least from the perspective of many people today, to tolerate different opinions and even to give in for the sake of unity and harmony. However, with millions of people dying or suffering from Long Covid, the question of how people are to behave under such circumstances becomes a serious public matter rather than simply a private one." Christoph Stenschke, "The 'Strong' and the 'Weak' in Romans 14:1–15:13 and Covid-19-Related Tensions in Christian Congregations: The Prospects and Perils of Relating Current Concerns to Sacred Scripture," *Neotestamentica* 57.1 (2023): 25–56 [37–38].

Stenschke's assessment reflects fundamental misunderstandings: of the coronavirus (not as deadly as portrayed, for the vast majority of people), of the effectiveness of the COVID vaccines (not protective against infection or transmission, such that everyone will eventually be exposed to COVID and in principle be at risk for so-called "Long COVID"). But most relevant here, he fails to grasp the dire spiritual seriousness of food-and-drink segregation, even in the face of physical risk: "For if we live, we live to the Lord, and if we die, we die to the Lord" (Rom 14:8a).

believers of the blessing of fellowship with their Jewish fellow believers in Jesus—and they had robbed God of the joy of seeing Jews and Gentiles worshipping together as "a testimony to the powers" that all peoples belong rightfully to Him. Godly leadership *insists* that no one may *insist* on conscience matters. To refrain from insisting in such a case constitutes a failure of shepherding that dishonors God.

Leaders who permitted morality to be restructured unbiblically to include "spread of disease" allowed outside forces to "spy on our liberty and bring us into bondage." Separating out unvaccinated individuals was tantamount to treating them as "unclean" vectors of disease (leaving aside the realities of natural immunity and the ineffectiveness of vaccines at preventing transmission—see Chapter 12). This approach shamed and manipulated others on amoral matters of conscience. Christians who chose to be vaccinated and tolerated segregation have made the same mistake as Peter: they might not have chosen the system, but because segregation did not punish them directly, they failed to defend the consciences of brothers and sisters who made a different choice than they did. Thus, they allowed Christ to be robbed of glory in His church unified.[35]

Personal Story: Solidarity, Empathy, and the Relational Harms of Tolerating Segregation

Some examples from my own experience living in a regime of segregation may illustrate these arguments and illumine the human impact of these shepherding errors.

---

35. Could white Christians who recognized the evil of racial segregation in the 1960s have been content with their own freedom to worship in either "whites-only churches" or racially-integrated churches? Certainly not—to tolerate the situation would make a white Christian a "bystander" to the evil of segregation.

I mentioned in Chapter 12 that the government in my country of residence instituted a regime of legal segregation between August 2021[36] and February 2022. In order to enter nearly all public indoor spaces: citizens and residents ages twelve and older needed to show an "opportunity pass," indicating one of the following: 1) up-to-date vaccination or booster (last seven months), 2) recovery from COVID within the last six months, or 3) sufficient antibodies in test within the last 60 days. This was not required for grocery stores, public transit, and (we later found out) houses of worship—but for nearly everything else: entertainment and dining, all non-grocery stores, and institutions of higher education.

It is difficult to convey to those who did not live under such restrictions just how degrading, divisive, demoralizing and inconvenient it was for this society and for communities within it. Even though I myself possessed the "opportunity pass" as a reward of recovery from COVID and continued antibody testing (every 60 days at my own expense), I chose to avoid any situation where it was required, as an expression of solidary with my friends and colleagues who did not have the pass. This entailed ordering many things online (navigating Lithuanian-language websites, an inconvenience for non-native speakers), and sometimes even sending my children (who were under age twelve at the time, and therefore exempt) into stores to make simple purchases.[37] I did end up using the "opportunity pass" one time to take my child into a mall to make some essential purchase. But I felt so disgusted

---

36. It should be noted that this was long after it was known that vaccination did not prevent contraction and spread of disease, so the "externalities" rationale could not have been legitimately argued; see Chapter 12.

37. This was not so strange in our country, where children enjoy a lot more freedom and autonomy than in the USA. On one occasion, I sent my son into a hardware store to buy a simple tool he needed for a school project—he was better off without me anyway, because he spoke the local language fluently and could ask for what he needed.

about having to "show my papers" (i.e., a QR code on my phone) in order to enter a store, that I resolved never to do it again.

This regime meant that, in Fall 2021, unvaccinated students were excluded from in-person university campuses. At that time, I was resigned to continue teaching my in-person classes "under protest," for the sake of the students who had submitted to the requirements. (I continued to teach an online section and in "hybrid format" for the sake of students who were stuck in their home countries, unable to travel.)

But I pleaded with the Student Life office to move our Friday chapel services outside (weather permitting) or to a local church building, where the rules did not apply. I made the same case to the leaders of a faculty-led Sunday evening worship service that was very special to our family. Sadly, neither leadership team saw the importance of this move to avoid segregating *worship* according to health status (which, to me, was a degree more outrageous even than segregating a *classroom*).

It is impossible to adequately communicate the disappointment that many students shared with me, that their Christian university (however bound by unjust and ineffective government requirements) did not take any kind of stand in support of their personal decision and the principle of medical freedom. (I did approach the administration about this, but there was no interest—they said I was free to make a statement on my own.) In intra-faculty conversations about such students, the tone of my colleagues' comments typically ranged from silence and eye-rolling, to exhaustion, frustration, and even explicit contempt for them.

I promised my unvaccinated students that I would never participate in a Christian worship service from which they would be excluded on the basis of health status, and so I and my family did not attend chapel services from August 2021 until February 2022 when the requirements were lifted (due to the spread of the omicron variant).[38] My children were disappointed not to attend the Sunday night services, which were very special to them—that was our regular opportunity to worship in English, and it was the fellowship in which each of my children had first received communion. But they both immediately understood the urgency of this act of solidarity with those who would have been turned away, and embraced it.

We (faculty and students who did not want to get vaccinated, or who found the requirements outrageous) would not have felt so betrayed and alienated, if only our vaccinated colleagues and friends (nearly all were Christians) would have acknowledged the situation and expressed some empathy and solidarity. A few colleagues did express solidarity, and I will forever be grateful for their understanding and loyalty. The institution also could have taken a public stance critical of medical coercion[39] while still complying. But there was no willingness to use our public influence to take a stand on these issues, even while the segregation regime and the "remote learning" undermined our educational model and mission.[40]

On the other hand, our small Lithuanian church was remarkably unified in taking a sensible, principled approach to managing risk in community. Masks were optional, but I chose to wear one

---

38. The "opportunity pass" system was discontinued in Lithuania soon thereafter, though the EU certificate (required for travel to other countries without an isolation period) remained in place until August 2022.

39. Not to mention the restrictions on migration and travel—not only were the restrictions quite onerous to our highly-international community, migration studies was also explicitly named in our institutional research agenda as a field of special emphasis.

40. And, this was not a case of lack of voice in the country. The university's president was a frequent guest of the American and Canadian embassies in Vilnius, and regularly met with government officials and NATO officers. Nor was the silence due to a principled commitment to institutional neutrality or silence on controversial issues. During the Summer of 2020 (i.e., during the pandemic), the faculty, staff and students were encouraged to take part in a Lithuania-wide demonstration of solidarity with democratic reformers in Belarus (which I did, based on shared conviction). But the institution could have offered a measured, thoughtful statement to the parliament, speaking out against lockdowns in the midst of a mushrooming mental health crisis, and for medical autonomy and the freedom to cross borders, based on principles of Christianity and Western liberalism—but no statement was forthcoming.

when serving communion. We had a mix of vaccinated, recovered, and "naïve" (i.e., never had COVID) persons—and there was never any talk of checking passes or turning people away from worship. In God's providence, many of us younger people got COVID and recovered before vaccines were even available, which left us with a degree of "herd immunity" that made the older people feel much safer (though not without some risk). No church is perfect, but it truly was a joyful place of worship and community, a refuge for our family.

Denying Denial

It is crucial that Christian leaders not look away from these harms done to their people by these measures described, especially segregation of worship. In addition to the spiritual harms to Christian communities listed in this chapter, there were the social and emotional harms of separation, alienation, and resentment (in both directions—the vaccinated toward the unvaccinated, and viceversa) that were allowed to fester. Discerning leadership could have stabilized churches by insisting on freedom of conscience.

Many people were alienated from the church during this time, due to these factors. Some of them found other churches (a selfsort), but others have yet to return to church. As with any church split, it is easy for those who stay to forget about those who departed—eventually, the community takes on a different identity. But "out of sight, out of mind" is not a responsible pastoral strategy toward those who perceive spiritual harm done to them.

CHAPTER 15 | Christian Leadership Failures

As a Christian leader (minister, professor, chaplain), I share responsibility to point out (and own-up to my part in) the failures that are particular to the church and Christian leadership. What were the mistakes made by Christians with public influence, including leaders of prominent churches and institutions? Here it is necessary to point out some general patterns of mistakes and blind spots on the part of prominent evangelical leaders whom I respect a great deal, in order to show how even principled, thoughtful people failed to recognize the dangers and distortions.

Failure to Recognize Spiritual Warfare

In retrospect, it is difficult not to see spiritual warfare behind these mistakes. Rebellious spiritual beings ("powers and authorities in the heavenly places," Eph 3:10; 6:12) have contempt for humans who are made in the image of God, and they love to see us divided against one another and separated by sin and fear (thus reflecting the image of God in a fractured and imperfect way). When authorities say to humans, "love each other by staying away from each other," pastors' "spider-sense" should be tingling—this could be demonic. When government authorities steamroll the consciences of people in their care, this is demonic because it abuses and degrades the image of God in all of us. By contrast, the example of our Savior is that he touched those who had diseases

(Luke 4:40), and girded himself with only a towel to wash his disciples' feet (John 13:1–15; see Chapter 7). Physical presence is necessary for love of neighbor.

Failure to Recognize Moralizing Distortions of True Law

In the previous chapter, I described the moralizing language that surrounded COVID infection in the first year (and declining vaccination in subsequent years), as well as the immorality of segregating churches on the basis of masks or vaccination. It bears exploring how the distortion of moralizing illness paved the way for segregation.

Moralizing the illness was based on a "law" which divided people into moral "law-keepers" and immoral "scofflaws." The "law" was the notion that through responsible behavior one could have avoided becoming infected with COVID. Thus, Group A were those who loved their neighbors by behaving responsibly: avoiding contact with others, or having contact only with other responsible people from Group A.

What then was implicitly communicated concerning Group B, people who took more risks for various reasons (fellowship, mental health, lack of concern about their personal risks of COVID)? They would tend to be viewed by those in Group A as irresponsible and immoral. This moral outrage would then become indignation and anger on behalf of those from Group A (or people whose essential jobs put them in the path of the disease— they had little choice) who got COVID. Group A people could say, "My law-keeping went unrewarded, because these others were irresponsible!"

This moral opprobrium pertaining to something that was ultimately not a moral "law" (because everyone eventually contracted the disease, and disease itself is amoral) was transferred to something that was indeed a choice: to wear a mask or not, and later, to take a vaccine or not. Prior to 2020, a small minority of citizens declined standard childhood vaccinations for various reasons, but this choice was not usually framed by the majority in moral terms. The moral framing of the false law of "healthy = moral; sick = irresponsible/immoral" opened the door for the framing of a new false law concerning masks and vaccinations. (This is a "false law" in that it does not comport with God's law revealed in scripture, *and* in that it turned out to be factually incorrect with respect to avoiding the disease.)

Church leaders who would normally reject segregation in principle, nevertheless consented to the demands of some members (or authorities) that services be segregated. This leads to the question: Is segregating brothers and sisters who choose to decline a COVID vaccine an act of obedience to 1 Corinthians 5—i.e., these brothers and sisters are sinning by not getting the vaccine and thus the rest of the church withdraws the hand of fellowship as an act of discipline to prompt repentance?

While some extremely zealous leaders would hold this position, most pastors would not venture so far as to say that refusing the vaccine is a moral sin. But if it is not a sin, then what justification could there be for enforcing separation, or penalizing people? In fact, segregating some members due to the incorrect beliefs of other members (i.e., "If others around me are vaccinated, I won't contract the virus") is more akin to the situation in Galatians 2: segregation of Gentiles away from Jews. Vaccinated Christian leaders who failed to stand up for their unvaccinated brethren are guilty of the same sin as Peter and the other apostles whom Paul corrects.

Scientism and Respectability Anxiety

Another significant error, which must be reflected upon, is that Christian leaders were too trusting of secular authorities, including government, the top of the medical establishment, and academic structures that claim to generate actionable knowledge about the world. It is this subject that will occupy most of the remainder of this chapter, and Chapter 16.

Many evangelical elites who commendably strive to provide a winsome witness in the world, are troubled about the broader society's perception of evangelical Christians as anti-intellectual and anti-science. These concerns are not entirely unfounded. One response on the part of Christian intellectuals is to elevate and promote individuals of Christian faith who are prominent and respected in the broader culture due to success in the scientific domain—thereby "proving" that Christians *can indeed* be good scientists.[1] This pattern becomes problematic, insofar as it relies *ad hominem* on the respectability, credibility and fidelity of individuals as ambassadors, rather than on logical argument.[2]

Megan Basham has reported on the government's apparently cynical manipulation of Christian leaders who then spread information (Basham regards it as "propaganda," and it is hard to disagree with that characterization) in support of the government's narratives on COVID.[3] This messaging included: criticism of the lab-leak hypothesis of the virus's origins;[4] promoting obedience to church closure orders; and, promoting masks—and later, vaccines—as

---

1. See the discussion in Chapter 4 about epistemological frameworks and what it takes to be "a good scientist." A professing Christian's professional success in the realm of scientific research is not sufficient to prove that the Christian faith is a "reasonable" worldview by the standards of modern rationalism, any more than the success of a scientist who is an atheist disproves the existence of God.

2. An appropriate analogy might be the tendency among evangelicals to immediately elevate and promote celebrity entertainers or athletes who profess faith in Christ—in so doing, we set ourselves up for ridicule when such figures display understandable ignorance of their new-found faith, or lack of sanctification (i.e., they make baby-Christian mistakes).

3. Megan Basham, "How the Federal Government Used Evangelical Leaders To Spread COVID Propaganda To Churches," *Illinois Family Institute*, 2 February 2022, originally published on DailyWire.com <https://illinoisfamily.org/religious/how-the-federal-government-used-evangelical-leaders-to-spread-covid-propaganda-to-churches/>.

4. Nicholas Wade, "A Covid Origin Conspiracy? Newly released emails make more plausible the contention that Anthony Fauci and Francis Collins presided over the suppression of the lab-leak theory for political reasons," *City Journal*, 23 January 2022 <https://www.city-journal.org/article/a-covid-origin-conspiracy>.

obedience to the biblical command to love one's neighbor. Francis Collins, a self-described evangelical Christian who was head of the National Institutes of Health (NIH), was chosen as an ambassador over someone like Anthony Fauci, because Collins had relationships and credibility within evangelicalism, particularly elite circles.

Christian leaders responded by promoting Francis Collins and the government's preferred policies. In numerous conversations with pastors and influential Christian leaders, Collins advocated adherence to the government's regulations, using Christian language. Those leaders, in turn, praised Collins while dismissing or even denigrating fellow Christians who objected on various grounds.

Rick Warren, the founding pastor of Saddleback Church and author of many books including *The Purpose Driven Life*, is to be commended for his careful avoidance of even the appearance of sexual impropriety through his personal "elevator rule," as well as his and his wife's decision to "reverse-tithe" ninety percent of their earnings from his successful books. Even Christians who are critical of some of the church-growth methods and movement that Warren has promoted should find much to admire about Warren. But in a videoconference broadcast with Collins during the COVID crisis, Warren promoted mask-wearing as "neighbor love," and with Collins, enjoined religious leaders to convince their people to accept government's narratives regarding COVID origins, masks, and vaccines:

> Warren and Collins spent their interview jointly lamenting the unlovingness of Christians who question the efficacy of masks, specifically framing it as a matter of obedience to Jesus. "Wearing a mask is the great commandment: love your neighbor as yourself," [Warren] declared…
>
> "Let me just say a word to the priests and pastors and rabbis and other faith leaders," he said. "This is our job, to deal with these conspiracy issues and things like that…

One of the responsibilities of faith leaders is to tell people to…trust the science. They're not going to put out a vaccine that's going to hurt people."[5]

Ed Stetzer is currently dean of Talbot School of Theology, has authored many influential books and articles about theology, the church, and missions, and has admirably led within influential Christian organizations and institutions, including Wheaton College, *Christianity Today*, LifeWay, and Outreach media group. But in a discussion with Collins, Stetzer likewise acquiesced to Collins and even encouraged pastors to weigh in on debatable issues (vaccination, child masking) on the side of government prescriptions:

During their discussion, Collins and Stetzer were hardly shy about the fact that they were asking ministers to act as the administration's go-between with their congregants. "I want to exhort pastors once again to try to use your credibility with your flock to put forward the public health measures that we know can work," Collins said. Stetzer replied that he sometimes hears from ministers who don't feel comfortable preaching about Covid vaccines, and he advises them, in those cases, to simply promote the jab through social media. "'I just tell them, when you get vaccinated, post a picture and say, 'So thankful I was able to get vaccinated,'" Stetzer said. "People need to see that it is the reasonable view."[6]

N.T. Wright, one of the most influential academic and public theologians of our time, and a bishop in the Church of England, has written about the anti-imperial dimensions of the gospel message that "Jesus is Lord (and therefore, Caesar isn't)," as well as the

5. Basham, "How the Federal Government Used Evangelical Leaders." Full conversation between Warren and Collins: <https://www.youtube.com/watch?v=Lz-WMXld0rk>

6. Basham, "How the Federal Government Used Evangelical Leaders." Full conversation between Stetzer and Collins: <https://www.youtube.com/watch?v=2JnGZpldjT8>

importance of knowing through rituals such as the sacraments (see my discussion in Chapters 3–4, heavily reliant on Wright's thinking). But in a discussion with Collins, his personal friend, Wright accepted the government's narratives, and even caricatured fellow Christians who were suspicious of government overreach into the church:

> During a discussion where the NIH director once again trumpeted the efficacy of cloth masks, the pair warned against conspiracies, mocking "disturbing examples" of churches that continued meeting because they thought "the devil can't get into my church" or "Jesus is my vaccine." Lest anyone wonder whether Wright experienced some pause over lending his reputation as a deep Christian thinker to Caesar's agent, the friends finished with a guitar duet.[7]

The late Tim Keller was pastor emeritus of Redeemer Presbyterian Church in New York City and author of dozens of important books advocating the reasonableness of faith in Christ in a skeptical age—a pastoral and theological giant of the turn of the century. But Keller's friendship with an elite scientist such as Francis Collins led him to slander a fellow pastor who took a different approach than Keller would have (he retired from the pastorate at Redeemer in 2017, prior to COVID):

> …Keller's joint interview with Collins included a digression where the pair agreed that churches like John MacArthur's, which continued to meet in-person despite Covid lockdowns, represented the "bad and ugly" of good, bad, and ugly Christian responses to the virus.[8]

---

7. Basham, "How the Federal Government Used Evangelical Leaders." Full conversation between Wright and Collins: <https://www.youtube.com/watch?v=jhBGkdDhInE>

8. Basham, "How the Federal Government Used Evangelical Leaders." Full conversation between Keller and Collins: <https://www.youtube.com/watch?v=k2h3VEoL0d8>

These are just a few examples of Christian leaders who were misled by overreliance on their ostensibly respectable and reliable government source. Other publications such *Christianity Today* (CT) and The Gospel Coalition (TGC)[9] not only followed the "official" lines on pandemic measures, but even—strangely—on the origins of the virus. Basham observes:

> Much earlier in the pandemic, as an editor at evangelicalism's flagship publication, *Christianity Today* (*CT*), Stetzer had also penned essays parroting Collins' arguments on conspiracy theories. Among those he lambasted other believers for entertaining, the hypothesis that the coronavirus had leaked from a Wuhan lab. In a now deleted essay, preserved by Web Archive, Stetzer chided, "If you want to believe that some secret lab created this as a biological weapon, and now everyone is covering that up, I can't stop you." It may seem strange, given the evidence now emerging of NIH-funded gain-of-function research in Wuhan, to hear a church leader instruct Christians to "repent" for the sin of discussing the plausible supposition that the virus had escaped from a Chinese laboratory.[10]

It is not too difficult to understand why CT would have deleted Stetzer's op-ed, in light of credible evidence questioning zoonotic origin of the virus.[11] But hypotheses or speculation con-

---

9. Basham, "How the Federal Government Used Evangelical Leaders." "Certainly The Gospel Coalition, a publication largely written for and by pastors, didn't probe beyond the 'facts' Collins offered or consider any conflicts of interest the NIH director might have had before publishing several essays that cited him as almost their lone source of information. As with *CT*, one article by Gospel Coalition editor Joe Carter linked the reasonable hypothesis that the virus might have been human-made with wilder QAnon fantasies. It then lectured readers that spreading such ideas would damage the church's witness in the world."

10. Basham, "How the Federal Government Used Evangelical Leaders."

11. Ed Stetzer, "On Christians Spreading Corona Conspiracies: Gullibility is not a Spiritual Gift," *Christianity Today* blog, 15 April 2020 <https://web.archive.org/web/20200416092325/https://www.christianitytoday.com/edstetzer/2020/april/christians-and-corona-conspiracies.html>.

cerning the origin of the virus are not directly pastorally relevant to the practice of the church in relation to pandemic restrictions (closures, masks, segregation, etc.), so it is hard to see why Stetzer weighed in on this, other than that he was influenced by Collins.

Given all that has now come out about the scientific basis for these interventions, it is appropriate (even necessary) for these leaders and publications—whom I respect on many other matters—to reassess their trust in secular authorities and people like Francis Collins (who is a prominent Christian example, but by no means the only one).[12] Behind the scenes, we now know that Collins was complicit in slandering and censoring fellow medical experts as "fringe epidemiologists" deserving of "a swift and devastating takedown" (notably the Great Barrington Declaration authors, including a fellow Christian believer, Jay Bhattacharya of Stanford).[13] In doing so, Collins bears significant responsibility for shutting down public debate on debatable matters, and covering up NIH/ NIAID[14] funding for risky gain-of-function research at the Wuhan Institute of Virology. In a subsequent interview, Collins (who retired from the NIH at the end of 2021) admitted errors in handling pandemic-related matters, including a single-minded focus on controlling the virus while ignoring other harms[15]—but Collins

---

12. To my knowledge, at the time of publication, none of the Christian leaders mentioned here who promoted Collins as a reliable authority during the pandemic has made any statement qualifying or revising their earlier support of Collins. I have endeavored to uncover any change of perspective on the part of these leaders—if I have overlooked a subsequent statement, I sincerely apologize.

13. "How Fauci and Collins Shut Down Covid Debate," *WSJ Opinion*, The Editorial Board, 21 December 2021 <https://www.wsj.com/articles/fauci-collins-emails-great-barrington-declaration-covid-pandemic-lockdown-11640129116>.

14. The National Institute of Allergy and Infectious Diseases (NIAID) is a division of the NIH.

15. Collins recently admitted some failures: "…If you're a public health person and you're trying to make a decision, you have this very narrow view of what the right decision is, and that is something that will save a life, doesn't matter what else happens. So you attach infinite value to stopping the disease and saving a life. You attach a zero value to whether this actually totally disrupts people's lives, ruins the economy, and has many kids kept out of school…This is a public health mindset, and I think a lot of us involved in trying to make those recommendations had that mindset, and that was really unfortunate." Video excerpted on Twitter by Anthony Bradley <https://twitter.com/drantbradley/status/1740356605906919813>. See further quotations from Collins's remarks, and response by Bethel McGrew, "Francis Collins is Not Sorry Enough: Why I don't accept his apology," *Further Up* Substack, 5 January 2024 <https://www.furtherup.net/p/francis-collins-is-not-sorry-enough>.

has not, to my knowledge, repented of his coercive censorship, his unfair accusations of his fellow scientists and his Christian brothers and sisters, or his manipulation of Christian leaders.[16]

Why did Christian leaders respond so quickly and forcefully on the side of the government's narratives? I am willing to believe that most had good intentions, desiring to be responsible leaders promoting good citizenship. Sadly, other concerns often taint the agendas of Christian leadership. Carl Trueman has written compellingly about the anxiety of Christian (especially evangelical) elites to be perceived as respectable in the eyes of the world.[17] This is particularly true in matters related to science, where Christian elites display angst that Christians are perceived by outsiders as "anti-science";[18] and in the wake of the 2016 election of Donald

---

16. In his recent (September 2024) memoir, Collins expresses regrets about certain shortcomings and ineptness of the pandemic response; but he defends his efforts to censor the Great Barrington Declaration: "In a moment of deep concern, when I was admittedly intemperate with language in an email, I did suggest that something—'a quick and devastating takedown'—should be urgently undertaken to try to counter these recommendations, or many lives would be lost. (In retrospect, I have no regrets for the point I made, only for the manner in which I expressed it.) What was being promoted in the declaration was lethally wrong, and that is just as clear now as it was then. Wasn't it part of my job to sound the alarm when faced with recommendations that presented serious risks to innocent people, and that were being promoted at the highest level of government without any actual scientific debate? As far as I know, my intemperate private email had no effect on anyone, but in the rearview mirror it has been interpreted as the government trying to squash scientific discussion. It was no such thing." Francis S. Collins, *The Road to Wisdom: On Truth, Science, Faith, and Trust* (New York: Little, Brown and Company & Worthy Books, 2024), 110–111.

17. Carl R. Trueman, "The Failure of Evangelical Elites," *First Things*, November 2021 <https://www.firstthings.com/article/2021/11/the-failure-of-evangelical-elites>; Trueman, "Faithfulness Is the Future of the Church," *Religion & Liberty* 32.3, 5 July 2022 <https://www.acton.org/religion-liberty/volume-35-number-3/faithfulness-future-church>. See also, interestingly on TGC: Brett McCracken, "Beware the Corrosive Quest for Respectability," *The Gospel Coalition* blog, 20 September 2023 <https://www.thegospelcoalition.org/article/corrosive-quest-respectability/>.

18. Most notably, Mark Noll devotes chapter 7 of his influential book *The Scandal of the Evangelical Mind* (Grand Rapids: Eerdmans, 1994) to the history of evangelical thinking about science from the nineteenth century to the late twentieth century. He laments: "Under the social pressures of the early twentieth century as well as the impetus of their own movement, fundamentalists gave in to the weaker elements of their theology, with harmful results for the practice of science. In particular, fundamentalism retreated to Manichaeism, under the assumption that science was a battlefield in which the forces of light must yield nary an inch to the forces of darkness. It adopted a form of super supernaturalism, which had the effect of demonizing the ordinary study of nature. It also fastened on to notions of the 'literal interpretation' for the Bible that made it very difficult to see how earlier believers had found the Scriptures a stimulus to full-scale investigation of the physical world. The rise and, from the perspective of the nineteenth century, surprising strength of scientific creationism among evangelicals is the best illustration of these inclinations."

Trump, which was lamented by many ostensibly conservative Christian leaders.[19]

Christian elites' anxiety over being viewed as "anti-science" has created a blind-spot: failure to recognize "scientism" as the religion of modernity and its empires. For Daniel's three friends in Babylon, or early Christians in the Roman empire, the publicly-expected idolatrous worship of other gods was in obvious contradiction to their faith—thus, resistance to the cultural/imperial religion, though immensely costly in practice, was not theologically confusing. By contrast, science as an endeavor is fully compatible with Christian faith, part of the human vocation to discover and steward God's creation—thus, it is easier for Christians to miss the bait-and-switch that happens when cultural leaders begin to claim that the scientific method can provide not just provisional knowledge but also meaning and morality.[20]

Some Christian leaders responded to the situation in support of the government's narratives[21] with what may be charitably described as sophisticated answers to irrelevant (or less relevant) questions. Talbot, for example, in making the case for Christians to take the COVID vaccines, made a biblical case merely for the

---

19. This wedge between conservative and Christian elites and the broader conservative and Christian constituencies with respect to Donald Trump as a symbol is all the more puzzling with respect to Trump's handling of the COVID-19 pandemic response during the first year of the pandemic (the final year of his first term in office). Both Trump's ardent supporters and his fierce detractors often forget that the official policies of Trump's administration included lockdowns and rushed vaccines—either due to Trump's own preferences or due to his failure as a leader to make the members of his administration conform to more reasonable policies. For an inside look into the first Trump administration's COVID policy process, see Scott W. Atlas, *A Plague Upon Our House: My Fight at the Trump White House to Stop COVID from Destroying America* (Bombardier Books, 2021).

20. James Wood, "The COVID Regime as Stoicheic Order," *Theopolis*, 21 September 2021 <https://theopolisinstitute.com/the-covid-regime-as-stoicheic-order/>; Sheldon Richman, "How Science Becomes Religion," *The Libertarian Institute*, 30 July 2021 <https://libertarianinstitute.org/articles/sheldon/tgif-how-science-becomes-religion/>.

21. In support of the UK government's imposition on the Church, Richard A. Burridge, a respected NT scholar and a leader in the Church of England—ostensibly a sacramental church—wrote a book justifying the practice of "remote communion": *Holy Communion in Contagious Times: Celebrating the Eucharist in the Everyday and Online Worlds* (Eugene, OR: Cascade Books, 2022).

permissibility of using medicine and technology to improve human life.[22] Yet, virtually no Christians were questioning whether medicines *in general* are permissible—only whether this medicine should be *required* by the force of law or church discipline. Similarly, N.T. Wright, the theologian who has had more influence on my thinking than any other, contributed a book about the problem of natural evil in a broken world,[23] an issue which has been wrestled with by philosophers, theologians, and lay people since ancient times. Well-known theologian and pastor John Piper (another author from whom I have personally learned a great deal) offered his theological analysis from a similar standpoint: suffering due to SARS-COV-2 and the accompanying restrictions reflects the groaning of a creation broken by human sin.[24]

But the issue of whether zoonotic spillover or human error (irresponsible, reckless and possibly illegal research) was responsible for SARS-COV-2 was more relevant for understanding the evolution of the virus and how to avoid similar catastrophes in the future—this was left to mostly atheist scientists and secular organizations to pursue and uncover.[25] Talk of gain-of-function origins was dismissed as "conspiracy theorizing" or racism/xenophobia. Christian thinkers and leaders such as those mentioned in this chapter could have used their vast intellect and moral courage

22. Mark Talbot, "The Bible and COVID Vaccines," *Center for Pastor Theologians* blog, 16 September 2021 <https://www.pastortheologians.com/articles/2021/9/16/the-bible-and-covid-vaccines>.

23. N.T. Wright, *God and the Pandemic: A Christian Reflection on the Coronavirus and Its Aftermath* (Grand Rapids, MI: Zondervan, 2020).

24. John Piper, *Coronavirus and Christ* (Wheaton, IL: Crossway, 2020), 61–62. (Open access: <https://document.desiringgod.org/coronavirus-and-christ-en.pdf?ts=1586278809>.)

25. Zach Weissmueller, "Do New Documents Prove a COVID Lab Leak?" *Reason*, 1 February 2024 <https://reason.com/podcast/2024/02/01/do-new-documents-prove-a-covid-lab-leak/>. Early on, see the work of the group DRASTIC: Rowan Jacobsen, "Exclusive: How Amateur Sleuths Broke the Wuhan Lab Story and Embarrassed the Media," *Newsweek*, 2 Jun 2021 <https://www.newsweek.com/exclusive-how-amateur-sleuths-broke-wuhan-lab-story-embarrassed-media-1596958>; Alina Chan and Matthew Ridley, *Viral: The Search for the Origin of COVID-19* (New York: Harper, 2021).

to advocate for freedom, transparency and accountability—a missed opportunity, to put it mildly.[26]

Evangelical members of elite circles (media, academia, government, big business) craving the respect of the world (and I myself am guilty of this, as I will confess below) are all too eager to disassociate ourselves from our "lay" Christian brethren: "We're not like those nutty 'fundamentalists'! We're the responsible, sensible ones who can be reasoned with."[27] The danger is that we become too enthralled to the world.[28] I have thus far been critical of several leaders for whom I have great respect and from whom I have learned a great deal, including Warren, Stetzer, Keller, Wright, and Piper.[29] Conversely, there are many Christian lead-

---

26. Certainly not speech "according to the need of the moment, giving grace to those who hear" (Eph 4:29).

27. Carl R Trueman, "'Yes, I am a Christian, just like those over there': Standing with humble believers against the demands of a decadent culture," *World* Opinions, 27 January 2023 <https://wng.org/opinions/yes-i-am-a-christian-just-like-those-over-there-1674821578>.

28. See, for example, the attitudes expressed by evangelicals who were coauthors on the study reported by Brian McNeill, "Evangelical Christians were less likely to get COVID-19 vaccine after conversations with faith leaders," *VCU News* blog, 28 September 2022 <https://news.vcu.edu/article/2022/09/evangelicals-were-less-likely-to-get-covid-19-vaccine-after-conversations-with-faith-leaders>. "Gina A. Zurlo, Ph.D., co-director of the Center for the Study of Global Christianity at the Gordon-Conwell Theological Seminary and co-author of the study, said the study is 'important because it puts facts behind a common refrain from the media over the past two years—that evangelical Christians are anti-vaccination.'

"'While it is true that, generally, this group of people are vaccine hesitant, our study revealed more nuance related to age, family status and rural/urban dynamics,' Zurlo said. 'Furthermore, this research helps religious leaders understand just how influential they are not only in their parishioners' spiritual health, but also their physical health.'"

29. This is not a unique phenomenon within the church, even though evangelicals are perhaps more susceptible. Certain "respectable" libertarians and anarchists, with whom I agree on many issues, nevertheless compromised their principles or missed the broader issues during COVID. Some particularly (to me) lamentable examples include Julian Sanchez, "Vaccine 'Passports' Could Be Useful—but Only If Government Gets Out of the Way," *Cato.org*, 11 April 2021 <https://www.cato.org/commentary/vaccine-passports-could-be-useful-only-government-gets-out-way>; Ilya Somin, with Kevin L. Cope and Alexander Stremitzer, "Vaccine Passports as a Constitutional Right," *Arizona State Law Journal* 51 (2022) <https://papers.ssrn.com/sol3/papers.cfm?abstract_id=3910194>; Noam Chomsky, as reported on Twitter by Max Blumenthal: "Noam Chomsky says the 'right response' to The Unvaccinated is 'to insist that they be isolated' from society," 2 September 2021 <https://x.com/MaxBlumenthal/status/1433295789716086787>; "Noam Chomsky doubles down on his previous call for the state to segregate The Unvaccinated from society: 'How can we get food to them? Well, that's actually their problem,'" 25 October 2021 <https://x.com/MaxBlumenthal/status/1452490014533816323>.

ers with whose theological views or tone I have serious disagreements, who nevertheless took courageous but "non-respectable"
stances during COVID: John MacArthur, Sean Feucht, Mark
Driscoll, Douglas Wilson, Mark Dever, and James Coates,[30] to
name a few examples. Credit should be given where credit is due:
ultimately, churches that defied mandates or government pressure
(see Chapter 5), survived and even thrived.[31] Other churches suffered because they remained closed for months and/or introduced
divisive policies that segregated based on vaccination status (see
Chapter 14).[32]

Giving In to Fear and Competing *Teloi*

Scientism must be understood within the general modernist narrative of *progressivism* or the "myth of progress." If we believe that
society is shaped by the progress of technology and economic activity, it is easy to lured into a kind of techno-optimism or utopianism that assumes "things will always get better." Christians can
find themselves lured into progressivism, a form of utopianism,

30. Marnie Cathcart, "Alberta Pastor James Coates to Be Acquitted of All COVID Charges," *The Epoch Times*, 22 August 2023 <https://www.theepochtimes.com/world/alberta-pastor-james-coates-to-be-aquitted-of-all-covid-charges-following-court-decision-invalidating-cmoh-orders-5478704?rs=SHRNCMMW>.

31. Joel W. West, "Church Planting in Covidtide: Moral Courage and Sacramental Witness, Part I," *North American Anglican* blog, 28 July 2021 <https://northamanglican.com/church-planting-in-covidtide-moral-courage-and-sacramental-witness-part-i/>.

32. See the advice given by Daniel P. Chin, "Where Two or More Are Vaccinated: Advice for Churches in 2021. Five science-based suggestions to gather and worship safely as COVID-19 vaccines roll out," *Christianity Today*, 27 January 2021 <https://www.christianitytoday.com/ct/2021/january-web-only/church-reopening-vaccine-coronavirus-covid-advice.html>. Nearly all of the premises of Chin's prescriptions have been subsequently disproven. Even more pernicious is the moralizing effect of this advice on church communities: if congregational gathering is dependent upon how many in the congregation are vaccinated, and gathering for worship is a moral good (most agree on this), then the vaccinated will inevitably blame the unvaccinated for preventing the congregation from meeting. Alternatively, churches would segregate on the basis of vaccination, a possibility that Chin does not rule out.
On the other hand, Jamie Franklin has written an eloquent and strident case: "Radical Hospitality—A Theological Argument against Vaccine Passports in Churches," *Commentary on Faith and Current Affairs* blog, 31 August 2021 <https://jamiefranklin.wordpress.com/2021/08/31/radical-hospitality-a-theological-argument-against-vaccine-passports-in-churches/>.

because it purports to be amoral or compatible with a Christian *telos*.[33] The problems of the myth of progress for Christian belief are 1) the moral compromises along the way to progress; 2) the knowledge problem (see the discussion of Hayek in Chapter 16); and 3) the fact that a *telos* of "progress" will always emerge, and the prevailing *telos* will often be incompatible with the biblical *telos* of humanity, i.e., "to glorify God and enjoy Him forever" (WLC 1).

Alongside the phenomenon of *scientism*, we also see within Western society the progressivist impulse of *safetyism*, or the idolization of physical and emotional safety. We must acknowledge that prudence is a biblical virtue; Jesus quotes scripture to the devil, "You shall not put the Lord your God to the test" (Matt 4:7; cf. Deut 6:16). However, Jesus also spoke about the foolishness of one who stores up in barns but neglects his relationship with God (Luke 12:13–21).

Many Christians in the midst of COVID fell into the sin of idolizing safety and comfort. If I idolize safety and view it in moral terms, then anyone whom I perceive as a potential threat to my safety (through contact, not wearing a mask, or not taking a vaccine) becomes my moral and spiritual enemy.

Rather, scripture calls us to be wise and careful with the one earthly body that God has given each of us—but also to trust God in taking risks to serve others or bring glory to God. We make the mistake of thinking that God cannot use sickness and death for his glory—He can, and he does.[34]

---

33. See the discussion of *telos* in Chapter 4 of this book, "Science, Worship, and an 'Epistemology of Love.'"

34. John Piper has poignantly and boldly articulated how suffering in service to God brings God glory and is also good for us: John Piper, *Let the Nations Be Glad! The Supremacy of God in Missions* (Grand Rapids, MI: Baker Books, 1993), 87–112.

PART III

Healing, Repentance, Resilience

Part I made the case for the necessity of worship for human flourishing, and articulated concerns about the increasing technologization of worship, along with much of our communication. Part II articulated the church leadership failures of the COVID era, drawing on contemporary reporting and research, using the lens of leadership in Ezekiel as a heuristic.

Part III concludes this book on a positive (and ultimately hopeful) note, with constructive lessons from the COVID crisis. The silver lining of COVID is that it exposed many dysfunctional practices, attitudes, and underlying beliefs within the church (and in society), and has forced us to reevaluate. Chapter 16 articulates in brief a biblical case for principled humility on the part of elites with regard to what can be known by the scientific method. The biblical principle that should guide scientific research and human society is the *image of God*, which acknowledges our limitations and provides a moral framework that precludes censorship, manipulation, and coercion. Chapter 17 focuses on church practice and relationships: in light of all that has happened, how can churches pursue truth, repentance, and reconciliation? The issue is urgent, because "a house divided" (Matt 12:25; 1 Cor 1:10–17) or "a house built on sand" (Matt 7:26–27) will not long endure. Chapter 18 concludes with biblical hope for leaders who have stumbled, and for communities that have fractured.

CHAPTER 16 | Biblical and Scientific Resources for a More Robust Christian Response

The Bible must be our norm for belief and practice, and the Bible forms the foundation for all other knowledge about God's world. Through careful reasoning from the scriptures, we determined in Part I that knowledge through the rituals that God has given us, is genuine, actionable knowledge—an epistemology of love.

Additionally, through reason and common grace, social scientists have developed useful tools to understand how it is that the scientific enterprise is succeeding or failing at providing true, actionable information. In this section, we will briefly *survey* (not expound) some concepts that may help Christian leaders formulate a realistic, biblical, and faithful stance toward the public health establishment in the future.

Cracks in the Ivory Tower

First of all, Christian leaders need to recognize that the scientific process itself has flaws and limitations. Thoughtful scientists—Christian and non-Christian—are increasingly speaking about the dysfunctions of the processes that claim to produce knowledge and meaning (a la Ezek 8–9). Here are just a few terms and concepts that are worth further exploration for thoughtful Christians.

Across all academic disciplines and fields, there is a growing recognition that the peer-review and publication process is fatally flawed due to incentives for all involved: researchers, editors, reviewers, and publishers.[1] These problems plague the natural sciences, the medical sciences, the social sciences, and especially the humanities (my discipline).[2] In 2021, an editorial published in the *British Medical Journal* by the former editor suggested that it is "Time to assume that health research is fraudulent until proven otherwise."[3] Aside from outright fraud and fabrication of data, there is the practice of "p-hacking": running statistical regressions until a statistically-significant (i.e., publishable) result is found, but failing to report all the non-significant results that preceded the "interesting" result. This does not even account for the influence of research money from private interests (see below), which skews the process and the results in the direction of profitable interventions and products.

Another problem with the peer-review process is the group-think, or the narrowed range of allowable perspectives, that pervades academic communities.[4] This phenomenon extends into applied fields like medicine. (The "sociology of science" and the "sociology of medicine" are fields of inquiry and critique in their own right—these fields would not exist if the scientific processes

---

1. Adam Mastroianni, "The rise and fall of peer review: Why the greatest scientific experiment in history failed, and why that's a great thing," *Experimental History* Substack, 13 December 2022 <https://www.experimental-history.com/p/the-rise-and-fall-of-peer-review>; Joakim Book, "Why So Much Science is Wrong, False, Puffed, or Misleading," *The Daily Economy*, 24 September 2020 <https://thedailyeconomy.org/article/why-so-much-science-is-wrong-false-puffed-or-misleading/>.

2. John P. A. Ioannidis, "Why Most Published Research Findings Are False," PLoS Med. 2005 Aug 30;2(8):e124 <https://doi.org/10.1371/journal.pmed.0020124>; "Replication Crisis," *Psychology Today*, n.d. <https://www.psychologytoday.com/us/basics/replication-crisis>.

3. Richard Smith, "Time to assume that health research is fraudulent until proven otherwise?" *BMJ Opinion*, 5 July 2021 <https://blogs.bmj.com/bmj/2021/07/05/time-to-assume-that-health-research-is-fraudulent-until-proved-otherwise/>.

4. Demonstrated notably by three academics in the so-called "Grievance Studies Project," *New Discourses*, n.d. <https://newdiscourses.com/grievance-studies-project/> (accessed 3 December 2024).

were always purely, rigorously "scientific" in an ideal sense, with no human foibles.[5]) During the pandemic, as scientists and medical professionals were socialized into certain rituals and practices that may not have made sense,[6] it became difficult for them to acknowledge that their field was corrupted and on some questions they were essentially flying blind.[7]

At the small university at which I taught until 2022, there were two natural science professors, and one instructor in another field who happened to also be trained as a nurse. Even after the omicron-variant wave had passed and the mask mandate was lifted in our country (February–March 2022), the last two people on campus who wore masks were the nurse and one of the science professors.

My initial reaction to these two colleagues was un-Christlike: condescension and disgust. But later, that changed to empathetic pity—it would be tremendously difficult, as a scientist or a nurse, to admit that scientists and medical professionals could have insisted on masks for two years despite their ineffectiveness. Upon further reflection, I reached an unsettling assessment of my own practice as an Old Testament professor and researcher. It is certain that a portion of the "insights" that I write and teach, I do so not because they are firmly established by evidence and argumentation, but because I would be ostracized as an Old Testament scholar if I did not affirm them. I might even feel like a traitor to

---

5. Classic works include Thomas S. Kuhn, *The Structure of Scientific Revolutions* (Chicago: University of Chicago Press, 1962); Michael Polanyi, *Personal Knowledge: Towards a Post-Critical Philosophy* (Chicago: University of Chicago Press, 1974). See also Peter Conrad, *The Medicalization of Society: On the Transformation of Human Conditions into Treatable Disorders* (Baltimore: Johns Hopkins University Press, 2007); Ann Bauer, "I Have Been Through This Before," *Tablet*, 27 October 2021 <https://www.tabletmag.com/sections/arts-letters/articles/i-have-been-through-this-before-bauer>.

6. See the discussion of "knowing through ritual" in Chapters 3 and 4.

7. Thomas Harrington, "The Treason of the Healers," *Brownstone Institute*, 26 October 2021 <https://brownstone.org/articles/the-treason-of-the-healers/>; Michael Tomlinson, "The Universities Failed Us During the Pandemic," *Brownstone Institute*, 1 September 2022 <https://brownstone.org/articles/the-universities-failed-us-during-the-pandemic/>.

the guild, or fear that my field is not fundamentally *wissenschaft-lich* or rigorous—a sobering possibility.[8]

Public Choice, Expressive Voting, Regulatory Capture

During the COVID-19 pandemic, why was the political process in ostensibly democratic countries not more responsive to the needs of the public? Important theories from political science and political economy help us to understand the apparent dysfunctions of elected officials and appointed regulators: public choice, expressive voting, and regulatory capture.

"Public choice applies the theories and methods of economics to the analysis of political behavior…"[9] Some of the key insights of public choice theory are that elected leaders are rational actors who respond to incentives, not mere avatars of the democratic will; and that there is no single democratically-determined "will of the people"—individuals have preferences, act, and vote; votes are aggregated to elect representatives, but the representatives then act in ways that no individual voter chose.

Fundamentally, this theory seeks to explain why elected officials (and those they appoint) often act at odds with the public interest, and why voters vote for policies that turn out to be contrary to the public good. Voters are not experts, so they vote for leaders who will represent them and choose public servants with relevant expertise. One key insight of public choice is "rational ignorance" with respect to voting—Caplan aptly summarizes:

---

8. I grapple with this possibility in the conclusion of my recent book: Benjamin D. Giffone, *Storymaking, Textual Development, and Varying Cultic Centralizations: Gathering and Fitting Unhewn Stones* (FAT II 142. Tübingen: Mohr Siebeck, 2023), 235–236.

9. William F. Shughart II, "Public Choice," *Concise Encyclopedia of Economics*, n.d. <https://www.econlib.org/library/Enc/PublicChoice.html>.

Time is money, and acquiring information requires time. Individuals balance the benefit of learning against its cost. In markets, if individuals know too little, they pay the price in missed opportunities; if they know too much, they pay the price in wasted time. The prudent path is to find out enough to make a tolerably good decision. Matters are different in politics. One vote is extraordinarily unlikely to change an election's outcome. So suppose an ignorant citizen votes randomly. Except in the freak case where he casts the decisive vote, flipping an otherwise deadlocked election, the marginal effect is zero. If time is money, acquiring political information takes time, and the expected personal benefit of voting is roughly zero, a rational, selfish individual chooses to be ignorant.[10]

Having articulated this standard logic, Caplan also adds the notion of a "rational irrationality": an individual voter has not merely the incentive to remain uninformed and vote randomly, but rather to indulge irrational (as well as ignorant) beliefs in expressive voting. If my vote does not affect my life directly, I will vote for what makes me feel good to have voted for it.[11]

It is not the point to reproduce this vast academic field. There is a robust literature that can be used to explain why public health authorities do not always have the public's best interests as their sole interest, or why they have a narrow understanding of "public

---

10. Bryan Caplan, *The Myth of the Rational Voter: Why Democracies Choose Bad Policies* (Princeton: Princeton University Press, 2006), 94.

11. Randall G. Holcombe, *Following Their Leaders: Political Preferences and Public Policy* (Cambridge Studies in Economics, Choice, and Society; New York: Cambridge University Press, 2023), 20–38.

interest."[12] Once a public health establishment exists as a bureaucracy, their job is to remain employed by justifying their continuing existence—not merely to advance public health.[13]

Another application of public choice is the recognition of the phenomenon of "regulatory capture," private actors seeking to influence the regulators who regulate their industries.[14] This is clearly a factor in the approval process for drugs and treatments, and why government agencies worked hand-in-hand with industry to present one set of solutions for the COVID pandemic (vaccines and patented treatments, not off-patent drugs). Vaccines were very profitable for the companies that made them, with government contracts to purchase their products for billions of dollars. It would be foolish to assume that pharmaceutical companies would *not* lobby regulators to purchase, promote, and mandate their products—and to indemnify the companies against lawsuits for harms resulting from their vaccines.[15] These unhealthy relationships and incentives existed long before the COVID-19 pandemic; for example, *Der Spiegel*'s reporting describes how pharmaceutical companies lobbied the World Health Organization to declare the 2009 swine flu (H1N1) outbreak to

---

12. As previously cited in Chapter 15, NIH Director Francis Collins later admitted that his single-minded focus on controlling the virus resulted in other societal harms: "…You attach infinite value to stopping the disease and saving a life. You attach a zero value to whether this actually totally disrupts people's lives, ruins the economy, and has many kids kept out of school…This is a public health mindset, and I think a lot of us involved in trying to make those recommendations had that mindset, and that was really unfortunate." Video excerpted on Twitter by Anthony Bradley <https://twitter.com/drantbradley/status/1740356605906919813>.

13. John Tierney, "Keeping Fear Alive: Reluctant to set the public free, policymakers and the public-health bureaucracy set unachievable and unnecessary goals," *City Journal*, 23 August 2021 <https://www.city-journal.org/article/keeping-fear-alive>; Jeffrey H. Anderson, "The Masking of America: Faceless people make compliant subjects, not good citizens," *Claremont Review of Books*, Summer 2021 <https://claremontreviewofbooks.com/the-masking-of-america/>.

14. Aseem Malhotra, "Curing the pandemic of misinformation on COVID-19 mRNA vaccines through real evidence-based medicine - Part 2," *Journal of Metabolic Health* [Online] 5.1 (26 September 2022) <http://dx.doi.org/10.7759/cureus.57960>.

15. MacKenzie Sigalos, "You can't sue Pfizer or Moderna if you have severe Covid vaccine side effects. The government likely won't compensate you for damages either," *CNBC*, 23 December 2020 <https://www.cnbc.com/2020/12/16/covid-vaccine-side-effects-compensation-lawsuit.html>.

be a pandemic, which would have triggered automatic government purchases of their products.[16]

Alongside regulatory capture, the fact is that government is the largest provider of funding for healthcare in the US and many Western countries, and so government-generated schedules and standards dictate which procedures and drugs the government will pay for. The effect is that many medical and scientific professionals are constrained by "standard of care" and reimbursement requirements of Medicare, Medicaid, the Veterans' Affairs Bureau, and insurance companies. They might wish to treat patients with different drugs and procedures, but their hands are tied because the funding comes from government programs and heavily-regulated medical insurance companies. If doctors do not follow standards of care dictated by government boards, they can lose their licenses to practice or be successfully sued for malpractice. Many doctors had their licenses threatened for prescribing treatments other than vaccines during COVID;[17] conversely, many hospitals and medical practices were financially incentivized to count more COVID patients,[18] and to distribute vaccines.

---

16. "…In mid-May [of 2009], about three weeks before the swine flu was declared a pandemic, 30 senior representatives of pharmaceutical companies met with WHO Director-General Chan and United Nations Secretary General Ban Ki Moon at WHO headquarters. The official reason for the meeting was to discuss ways to ensure that developing countries would be provided with pandemic vaccine. But at this point in time the vaccine industry was mainly interested in one question: the decision to declare phase 6.

"Everything hung on this decision. At stake was nothing less than a move to supply large segments of the world's population with flu vaccine. Phase 6 acted as a switch that would allow bells on the industry's cash registers to ring, risk-free. That's because many pandemic vaccine contracts had already been signed. Germany, for example, signed an agreement with the British firm GlaxoSmithKline (GSK) in 2007 to buy its pandemic vaccine -- as soon as phase 6 was declared. This agreement could explain why Professor Roy Anderson, one key scientific advisor to the British government, declared the swine flu a pandemic on May 1. What he neglected to say was that GSK was paying him an annual salary of more than €130,000 ($177,000)."

"Reconstruction of a Mass Hysteria: The Swine Flu Panic of 2009," *Spiegel International*, 12 March 2010 <https://www.spiegel.de/international/world/reconstruction-of-a-mass-hysteria-the-swine-flu-panic-of-2009-a-682613.html>.

17. Pierre Kory, "The War on Doctors and Patients," *Brownstone Institute*, 27 January 2023 <https://brownstone.org/articles/war-on-doctors-patients/>.

18. Mindy Casso, "Government pays hospitals more money for Covid-19 patients than non-Covid patients," *KGNS News*, 28 March 2022 <https://www.kgns.tv/2022/03/28/government-pays-hospitals-more-money-covid-19-patients-than-non-covid-patients/>.

Aside from public choice and regulatory capture, there is also the problem of knowledge, recognized and described by Nobel economist F.A. Hayek as the "fatal conceit"[19] or "the pretense of knowledge."[20] Even if all actors in a system are rational and benevolent (which is never completely the case), no one person has the knowledge and insight to plan complex systems—knowledge of various facets of the system is dispersed. There are always shortcomings and unintended consequences. This does not mean that collective actions should never be undertaken, but that humility and caution are warranted.

These concepts are all consonant with biblical anthropology. The Bible teaches us that individuals are sinners but benefit from common grace: a mix of selfless and self-centered motives. Individuals may be self-deceived. Individuals have ideals or pragmatic concerns that do not match God's ideal or the common good as defined in God's Word. Individuals think they know more than they do, and attempt to engineer perfection that only God can achieve.

Christian leaders can find in these concepts—public choice, rational ignorance/rational irrationality, regulatory capture, the problem of knowledge—resources to keep public health officials' and political leaders' actions in proper perspective, and to balance them against the values of the spiritual needs of their communities, a holistic understanding of "the common good" and "neighbor love," and the dignity of individuals to live according to their own consciences.

---

19. F.A. Hayek, *The Fatal Conceit: The Errors of Socialism*, edited by W.W. Bartley III (Chicago: University of Chicago Press, 1988).

20. F.A. Hayek, "The Pretence of Knowledge," Nobel lecture, 11 December 1974 <https://www.nobelprize.org/prizes/economic-sciences/1974/hayek/lecture/>.

Censorship, Coercion, and Image-of-God Ethics

The pretense of comprehensive knowledge can lead authorities to justify surveillance[21] and censorship (see Chapter 13). Censorship, whether hard censorship backed by government force or soft censorship (see Chapter 9) by incentivizing media and tech companies to censor, exacerbates the problems of regulatory capture and public choice. As we saw previously, governments colluded with tech companies to create an illusion of a scientific consensus on many debatable issues. Thus, people were led away from closer understanding of truths that would have allowed them to act in the best interests of themselves and their families. Individuals, families, communities and societies were harmed as a result—more harmed than by supposedly "false" information being distributed.[22] Christian leaders should be leading the way in denouncing censorship and fostering debates that allow for different scientific views to be presented.

This imperative is rooted in the dignity of each human person as made in the image of God. The *imago Dei* is what makes us moral beings, accountable to God for what we do in our bodies (unlike animals, who act amorally according to mere instinct). Thus, each person has an imperative to make his/her own medical decisions and be accountable to God.[23] Each person should have freedom of conscience to speak, without threat of spiritual abuse or binding of consciences. Each person has the obligation from

---

21. Joseph Cox, "CDC Tracked Millions of Phones to See If Americans Followed COVID Lockdown Orders," *Vice*, 3 May 2022 <https://www.vice.com/en/article/m7vymn/cdc-tracked-phones-location-data-curfews>.

22. Matthew Crawford, "Covid was liberalism's endgame: Liberal individualism has an innate tendency towards authoritarianism," *UnHerd*, 21 May 2022 <https://unherd.com/2022/05/covid-was-liberalisms-endgame/>.

23. See the fifteen excellent reasons to support medical freedom presented by Rev. Holger Lahayne, "Galimybių pasas—moralė, teisė ir Bažnyčia" ("Opportunity Pass: Morality, Law and the Church"), *Laikmetis* opinion (Lithuanian), 21 September 2021 <https://www.laikmetis.lt/holger-lahayne-galimybiu-pasas-%D8%98-morale-teise-ir-baznycia/>.

our Creator to give Him praise, worshipping in community with other "images of God." Christian leaders who prevented worship, or who criticized/penalized other Christian believers who acted according to conscience on debatable issues, unwittingly undermined the ability of individuals to "live into" our human vocation as the image of God.

The significance of the *imago Dei* also needs to be understood in terms of bodily autonomy and medical ethics. Medical freedom is not about "demanding my rights" to do foolish things (thereby "putting YHWH your God to the test"). Medical freedom recognizes that each individual is given primary stewardship over his/her body before God and is therefore accountable to God for the things done with/in his/her body.[24]

Some who view the COVID vaccine as a personal or social good might respond that very few people in Western, liberal countries actually were *forced* to take vaccines. They would argue that it was a choice made by individuals to take the vaccine and retain their jobs (or scholarships, etc.), or to decline the vaccine and be dismissed—no one was restrained and forcibly injected.

No sensible person would argue, however, that a graduate student who covers up his professor's fraud because the professor has threatened to sabotage the student's career or frame the student for the fraud, or an actress who sleeps with a producer who controls the direction of her career, has done so *voluntarily*, in the sense of "euvoluntary" (i.e., truly voluntary).[25] Even though in each case the person technically had a choice (to conceal fraud, to sleep with the producer), their choices were made under duress.

---

24. "Primary stewardship" recognizes that parents have temporary stewardship over a child's body, and that old/infirm/incapacitated individuals are cared for by family members who sometimes make decisions for them. Even so, the previously-stated wishes of the incapacitated individual are used to guide the decisions made on their behalf, which is still an application/extension of their autonomy based in a respect for human dignity.

25. The term "euvoluntary" was coined by Michael C. Munger, "Euvoluntary or Not, Exchange Is Just," *Social Philosophy and Policy* 28.2 (2011): 192–211 <https://doi.org/10.1017/S0265052511000269>.

We recognize that such a professor or a producer would be guilty of abusing his or her position of authority.

In fact, indirect force was an explicit strategy used by many governments to coerce citizens into "voluntarily" (but not *euvoluntarily*) receiving the COVID vaccine. For example, Anthony Fauci, the head of the COVID response in the United States, stated in Summer 2021 that even though mandatory vaccination was not legally possible or politically feasible, universities and corporations could be convinced (or coerced by the threat of withholding federal funds) to require vaccination of their students and employees:

> I have to say that I don't see a big solution, other than some sort of mandatory vaccination. I know federal officials don't like to use that term. Once people feel empowered and protected legally, you're going to have schools, universities, and colleges are going to say, 'you want to come to this college buddy, you're going to get vaccinated. Lady, you're going to get vaccinated.' Yeah, big corporations, like Amazon and Facebook and all of those others, are going to say 'you want to work for us, you get vaccinated.' And it's been proven that when you make it difficult for people in their lives, they lose their ideological bullshit and they get vaccinated.[26]

One element of this strategy changing the Occupational Safety and Health Administration (OSHA) rules to require companies

---

26. Dr. Anthony Fauci in Summer 2021, as transcribed by US House of Representatives Committee on Oversight and Accountability, "Hearing Wrap Up: Dr. Fauci Held Publicly Accountable by Select Subcommittee," 4 June 2024 <https://oversight.house.gov/release/hearing-wrap-up-dr-fauci-held-publicly-accountable-by-select-subcommittee/>.

with one hundred or more employees to either require vaccinations or weekly COVID-19 tests.[27]

If COVID really were as transmissible and as deadly as, say, Ebola—and if the vaccines halted transmission—then arguably, based on the non-aggression principle, governments *should* have forbidden unvaccinated individuals to go even to grocery stores or on public transit—perhaps even locked people in their homes. The fact that in Western countries the authorities chose to use indirect force by threatening people's livelihoods demonstrates that the main objective was public compliance at a low political and financial cost.

It is correct, therefore, to view as victims those who were deprived of their *truly voluntary* choice to decline a vaccine. Self-stewardship is not "ideological bullshit," but the main principle (rooted in biblical truth) that guards against human abuse of others. What is the alternative to self-stewardship of the body? Coercion and force: someone else has authority over my body, can require me to make different risk/benefit tradeoffs than I would choose for myself, and can make decisions not based strictly on what is healthy for me, but on the basis of what might be good for themselves or some other group, or in service to some ideology. Taken to the logical extreme, we get the horrors of Soviet "science" and collectivist planning, the Nazis' dehumanizing experiments, the Tuskegee abuses, and other atrocities. It is these abuses that led to the Declaration of Helsinki, which enshrined the principle of *informed consent* as the cornerstone of medical ethics.[28] Looking back, one must say that the major intrusive interventions

---

27. Geoff Mulvihill, "Biden Administration Asks Court to Allow Vaccine Mandate," *The Associated Press*, 23 November 2021 <https://apnews.com/article/coronavirus-pandemic-business-health-occupational-safety-and-health-administration-bdc9a9881423cc03ca870038bb423bff>.

28. The Declaration of Helsinki is a code of ethics drafted by the World Medical Association, originally published in 1964, and revised several times subsequently. See "Human Experimentation: Code Of Ethics Of The World Medical Association—Declaration Of Helsinki," *British Medical Journal* 1964;2(5402):177 <https://doi.org/10.1136/bmj.2.5402.177>.

during COVID—lockdowns, masks, vaccines, and denial of early treatments—violated the principles of medical freedom and informed consent.

Ultimately: A Biblically Founded Philosophy of Science

In Chapters 1, 3, and 4, I described an epistemological shift in Western society, away from biblical authority as foundational for "knowing," and toward *empiricism* as the foundation of the scientific method. The thesis that I advanced was that "knowing through scripture" actually provides a firm theoretical foundation for the scientific method. Without such an objective foundation, empiricism is both theoretically weak and prone to overreach into the pursuits of *meaning* and *morality*.

In former NIH director Francis Collins's recent memoir, *The Road to Wisdom*, he offers in a rather informal style (befitting the genre) several explanations of his personal attempts to reconcile the life of a natural scientist with the life of a Christian disciple lived according to biblical truth. He rightly affirms the existence of objective truth, in the face of postmodern skepticism.[29]

However, he exhibits little understanding of the different sorts of truth claims and how they might be verified or falsified. He uses several visualizations to describe knowledge (not unlike my attempts in Chapter 1).

One visualization Collins presents is concentric circles of truth, with "necessary truth" at the center, "firmly established facts" around that, "uncertainty" next, and finally the outside ring of "opinion."[30] In the circle of "necessary truths" he places mainly statements governed by the laws of mathematics, such as "2 +2 = 4." But in the "firmly established facts" category, he places such

---

29. Francis S. Collins, *The Road to Wisdom: On Truth, Science, Faith, and Trust* (New York: Little, Brown and Company & Worthy Books, 2024), 40ff.

30. Collins, *The Road to Wisdom*, 35.

statements as "the force of gravity follows an inverse square of the distance between two objects," "heavy cigarette smoking is associated with a significantly increased risk of cancer," and "Germany shares a border with France, and both are in Europe." These are all very different kinds of claims, covering different domains of knowledge and ways of "knowing."[31] Amazingly, he also places in this category of "firmly established facts" the following statement:

> The COVID mRNA vaccines proved in large-scale clinical trials in 2020 to be highly beneficial in preventing illness and death; but once millions of people were being vaccinated, rare cases of heart muscle inflammation (myocarditis, fortunately reversible) were noted in about 1 in 10,000 young men.[32]

This statement on its face has so many contestable and contingent elements to it, that regardless of some truth in it, it cannot be understood as the same *kind* of claim as the location of a nation-state called "Germany" or the gravitational constant.

Elsewhere, Collins describes beliefs or premises, visualizing them as "nodes" of knowledge connected in a web that is individual to each person. For him, the central nodes include statements such as, "my wife loves me," "the scientific method is a reliable way to discern truth about nature," and "Jesus died for me and was then literally raised from the dead."[33] All of these are propositions, as we saw back in Chapters 3 and 4, are different kinds of claims, verified in different modes of "knowing."

Finally, Collins later visualizes values (love, beauty, goodness, freedom, truth, family, faith) as pillars connected by a web.

31. Collins, *The Road to Wisdom*, 37.
32. Collins, *The Road to Wisdom*, 38.
33. Collins, *The Road to Wisdom*, 52.

Collins's cheerful consolation about the divisions of Western society is that most people share those pillars. So if a disagreement results from a different "web" of knowledge nodes, better to do the following:

> ...Step back from the areas of disagreement where you may both be caught up in your webs. Focus instead on the pillars that stand at a deeper level. Talk about the fact that we all care about our families, and we want our much-loved children and grandchildren to inhabit a beautiful planet where they can flourish. Then the tone of the discussion may lighten, and a fresh opportunity may emerge that can move the conversation from contentiousness to respect to insight. Maybe even to wisdom.[34]

Though as a strategy for calming a tense social situation this approach is wise, Collins makes no allowance here for different prioritizations of these "pillars," different understandings of their outworkings, or any shared foundation on which these pillars are based.

Even though I have been rather critical of Collins at various junctures, I do not intend to single him out for "a devastating takedown" (to borrow Collins's own words). In my personal experience, many scientists and academics who have Christian faith exhibit a similar mindset: the Bible is what gives me morality and purpose, and shows me how to be reconciled to God—but does not have direct authority over the domain of my formal inquiry or over my research agenda.

What is needed instead is a truly Christian, biblical philosophy of science that places different modes and means of "knowing" in biblical perspective. As with the other concepts highlighted in

---

34. Collins, *The Road to Wisdom*, 63–64.

this chapter, it is beyond my capability and the constraints of this book to fully expound a biblical philosophy of science. However, a few directions for further inquiry can be briefly stated.

Scientific inquiry, empirical method, is dependent upon *repeatability*, which is founded on the principle of the *regularity of matter*. However, as David Hume rightly observed: past observation is not itself a guarantee of the future.[35] Simply by observing that "the sun has risen in the east on the last ninety-nine mornings," one cannot categorically deduce that "the sun will not rise in the west on the one-hundredth morning." "...Hume did not deny that he or anyone else formed beliefs on the basis of induction; he denied only that people have any reason to hold such beliefs (therefore, also, no one can know that any such belief is true)."[36]

Hume's criticism applies not only to atheists who take the transcendental principle of *regularity of matter* as a given, but also to many Christians who in practice assume the "laws of science" as independent of God's decree, God's character, or God's existence. Poythress notes:

Christians have sometimes adopted an unbiblical concept of God that moves him one step out of the way of our ordinary affairs. We ourselves may think of "scientific law" or "natural law" as a kind of cosmic mechanism or impersonal clockwork that runs the world most of the time, while God is on vacation. God comes and acts only rarely through miracle. But this is not biblical. "You cause the grass to grow for the livestock" (Ps. 104:14). "He gives

---

35. Brian Duignan, "Problem of Induction," *Encyclopedia Britannica*, 30 May 2013 <https://www.britannica.com/topic/problem-of-induction>.

36. Duignan, "Problem of Induction."

snow like wool" (Ps. 147:16). Let us not forget it. If we ourselves recovered a robust doctrine of God's involvement in daily caring for his world in detail, we would find ourselves in a much better position to dialogue with atheist scientists who rely on that same care.[37]

To Hume's skepticism, the Christian has a biblical answer where the methodological naturalist (atheist) has none. The natural world behaves regularly and predictably, according to observable laws, because the Creator God has made it so, consonant with his character. The world is "the work of [his] fingers" (Ps 8:3); he made the creation "very good" (Gen 1:31); "The earth is the LORD's…he has founded it…and established it…" (Ps 24:1–2); "…he upholds the universe by the word of his power" (Heb 1:3). We as humans can observe and describe those laws, even though our minds our limited due both to our human finitude and to our "darkened understanding" after the Fall (Eph 4:17–19; Rom 1:18–32). God is capable of altering the observable rules of the visible creation he has made, as evidenced repeatedly in the Bible. The visible and invisible creation are intertwined (Col 1:16), and God sometimes allows the invisible to become visible. The creation is broken, in bondage to decay because of human sin (Rom 8:18–25). But God is also the Redeemer, who allows the promised "new creation" to impinge upon the present—what we observe as "supernatural" miracles, the most significant being the resurrection of Jesus as the "firstfruits" of new creation (1 Cor 15:20–28).

---

37. Vern S. Poythress, *Redeeming Science: A God-Centered Approach* (Wheaton, IL: Crossway, 2006), 28.

As we saw when examining Wright's *History and Eschatology* back in Chapter 4: the love of God as New-Creator (Redeemer)—knowable through scripture's revelation and through biblical ritual—is the steady love of the Creator and Sustainer of the natural world, which makes the world knowable through scientific inquiry.

CHAPTER 17 | Re-Forming Church Biblically

"Then I'll get on my knees and pray/We don't get fooled again." —Pete Townshend

Confronting Our Past

I have argued that Christian leaders' default position based on our understanding of the image of God (and biblical understanding of human sinfulness, and the limits of governance by imperfect people) should be: advocating for open exchange on scientific issues, and calling out censorship that harms the public. This is an issue of justice: ensuring that the weak, ignorant and poor are not exploited or manipulated by elites who think they "know better."[1]

Christian leaders need to reflect on the evidence of the course of COVID-19 and the response to it, and recognize just how many minority positions (even censored positions) have actually turned out to be true (see Chapters 12–13).[2] Thus, we might pay particular heed to experts who "got it right" in the face of social

---

1. "The Harms of Lockdowns, The Dangers of Censorship, And A Path Forward," *American Institute for Economic Research*, 12 April 2021 <https://www.aier.org/article/the-harms-o f-lockdowns-the-dangers-of-censorship-and-a-path-forward/>; Gary Sidley, "UK Government Use of Behavioural Science Strategies in Covid-Event Messaging: Responsibility and Communication Ethics in Times of 'Crisis,'" *AHPb Magazine for Self & Society* 11 (2023–24) <https://ahpb.org/index.php/gary-sidley-article/?doing_wp_cron=1711287793.0690999031066894531250>.

2. Finally, in 2024, the CDC acknowledged that COVID guidelines needed to change—many months and years after the public had gone back to normal: Sumathi Reddy, "It's Official: We Can Pretty Much Treat Covid Like the Flu Now. Here's a Guide," *The Wall Street Journal*, 1 March 2024 <https://www.wsj.com/health/wellness/covid-guidelines-2024-cdc-symptoms-contagious-cdefb6b8>.

and professional pressure, especially those who were willing to change their positions based on evidence.[3] Rather than simply trusting everything these experts say (that would be foolish, as they themselves assert), we should seek to emulate their heuristics in future crises.

We also need to call Christian leaders who compromised their leadership responsibilities in the ways that I have described (closing worship, segregating, binding consciences), and exhort them to repentance.[4] (Then, we must also praise those who genuinely do repent, such as Andrew Walker.[5]) Some leaders may be guilty of seeking human praise and respectability in the eyes of the world. Some gave in to fear, rather than protecting the flock (Ezek 34).

Some Christian leaders were intellectually lazy and did not do research for themselves. This is a harsh criticism, I admit. We

---

3. One can see the evolving perspectives of scientists and physicians such as Bret Weinstein and Heather Heying (Dark Horse Podcast), Vinay Prasad (UCSF), Jay Battacharya (Stanford), Martin Kulldorff (formerly of Harvard), John Campbell (retired from University of Cumbria), and Aseem Malhotra.

Joseph Fraiman admirably apologized to fellow doctors and scientists for his former antagonistic stance toward their views: Ian Schwartz, "Emergency Room Doctor: I Apologize To Great Barrington Declaration Proponents, You Guys Were Correct," *RealClearPolitics*, 7 March 2022 <https://www.realclearpolitics.com/video/2022/03/07/emergency_room_doctor_i_apologize_to_great_barrington_declaration_proponents_you_guys_were_correct.html>.

4. "There is a place for trusting institutions, but this seemed to go too far, especially when reasonable voices of critique were roundly dismissed and castigated as conspiracy theorists, many of whom have been subsequently vindicated. But even worse than this, many of these Christian leaders mediated the messaging that any dissent from the covid regime was a failure to love one's neighbor, thus binding the consciences of Christians and stoking division in the church." James R. Wood, "This Article is Not About Tim Keller: Interrogating Evangelistic Politics," *American Reformer*, 12 May 2022 <https://americanreformer.org/2022/05/this-article-is-not-about-tim-keller/>; James R. Wood, "Sheep, Wolves, and Fools: On the Perils of a Winsome Ministry," *American Reformer*, 4 October 2022 <https://americanreformer.org/2022/10/sheep-wolves-and-fools/>; John F. Naugle, "Remember, Man, Thou Art Dust," *Brownstone Institute*, 21 February 2023 <https://brownstone.org/articles/remember-man-thou-art-dust/>.

5. Recently, Andrew T. Walker has commendably repented of his earlier contention that Christians should take the vaccine based on "love of neighbor": "The Wax Nose of Neighbor Love," *Public Discourse*, 15 April 2024 <https://www.thepublicdiscourse.com/2024/04/93212/>. Walker rightly points out that the same reasoning he used could be applied to encompass under "neighbor love" nearly any policy preference, and is therefore both a distortion of truth and a logical shortcut: "'Love of neighbor' is an ad-lib or choose-your-own-adventure approach to Christian ethics. Take one's desired outcome and reason backward from it under the supposition that loving one's neighbor requires unfettered support for the cause at hand and, *voilà*, all ethical deliberation is complete."

cannot all be experts, and many of the experts were wrong, misleading, or correct-but-censored! With that "rational ignorance" caveat, a Christian leader's instinct should be to resist and question if someone appears to be trying to coerce or divide his or her flock.[6]

Christian leaders should have a unique voice in society, advocating for the importance of gathering in community to worship and serve the Triune God.[7] Secular authorities are unable to judge the benefits of being together for worship, because their calculus cannot factor in the blessing of obedience to God and communion with God in worship (see Chapters 2–5). Furthermore, Christian leaders can speak up in protection of the vulnerable in society by holding secular authorities accountable in their spheres of sovereignty.

Christian leaders should broaden their view of compassion and justice to include all dimensions of the public good. In an epidemic, this means having equal compassion for those who are spiritually and physically vulnerable due to isolation, not only for those who are vulnerable to an infection.

Christian leaders, as I have suggested in the previous section, should be aware of the limits of science and scientism, and the pressures in the public square/industry *as actually practiced* (using public choice theory). Smart shepherding is challenging, and it requires wisdom and study (i.e., discerning research).

Christian leaders need to guard the ability of the church to worship God, without segregation. Two of the means of grace—the sacraments, and the fellowship of the saints—require other humans to be present. In the COVID-19 crisis, "scientism" as an alternate ideology/religion threatened shut down the church, and

---

6. Jeffrey A. Tucker, "How Coercion Compromised the Vaccine," *The Brownstone Institute*, 28 March 2022 <https://brownstone.org/articles/how-coercion-compromised-the-vaccine/>.

7. "The Frankfurt Declaration of Christian & Civil Liberties," August 2022 <https://frankfurtdeclaration.com>.

later, to divide the body of Christ based on health status (Chapter 15). This needs to be denounced and repented of, just as Paul called out the other apostles who were segregating Jewish and Gentile believers at Antioch. Saying to people, "you can't come to church or sit in this area of the church if you're not vaccinated" was not only ineffective at preventing spread of COVID-19 (see Chapter 12), it was *wrong* and betrayed the gospel.

Finally, given all that has alienated people from the church, Christian leaders need to encourage people to return to church by repenting of actions that undermined community, promoting the benefits of community, and actively removing barriers to people attending church. I do think this can mean some restructuring of worship spaces to encourage fearful people to come, within reason.

Repentance, Revival, and Healing in the Gospel

If this presentation concluded only with harsh condemnation and strong prescriptions for next time—i.e., only 'law'—then it would not be truly biblical. The gospel, as I expounded in Chapter 11 from the book of Ezekiel (and will conclude in Chapter 18), is that God responds to confession and repentance with forgiveness.

In recent years, many Christian leaders have advocated for (and performed) acts of corporate repentance for the historic sins of racism and slavery, on behalf of denominations, churches, and other institutions. While some are critical of these actions, I maintain that corporate confession and repentance is biblical and healthy—provided that the penitence is sincere, and the community chooses to live in forgiveness, joy, and holiness going forward. In some cases, churches or denominations who sincerely perform rituals or services communicating repentance for past sins, such as racism, apathy towards the poor, or not caring about evangelism, have seen growth and renewal.

The crisis of COVID-19 and its aftermath present Christian leaders with an opportunity to model and lead repentance in our churches. Repentance must begin with acknowledging the truth about what happened, and that we as leaders are unworthy in ourselves to approach God (Ezek 20:3–4; see also Neh 1:6–7; 9:16–30; Isa 63:7–64:12) and to lead. We as leaders (I include myself in this confession) took some steps in fear and in ignorance that we now regret. In retrospect, some of those measures (closing worship altogether, segregating, spiritual abuse/manipulation) in our communities were not only ineffective at furthering the common good, but morally wrong. At the other extreme end of the spectrum, some Christian leaders and laity need to repent for breaking fellowship frivolously by refusing reasonable measures, especially early on.

In the future, we must resolve to act with greater wisdom toward authorities who threaten manipulation or coercion.[8] We should look to authorities that are humble in acknowledging what can and cannot be known about a situation. We must not bind consciences on issues that are debatable, thereby safeguarding the image of God in each human person. We must re-devote ourselves to preaching God's Word, making disciples, leading worship of the Triune God, and promoting biblical justice in a fallen world.[9]

If Christian leaders repent publicly and refocus on "building YHWH's house" (see Hag 1:9–11, quoted in Chapter 10), then churches will flourish! Churches that repent and reunite will bring more glory to God, as his people worship and receive His means of grace, together. I predict that this will include not only spiritual growth as relationships are restored and leaders and lay

8. Evita Duffy-Alfonso, "If You Were A Sheep During Covid, Admit You Were Wrong And Do Better Next Time," *The Federalist*, 15 July 2023 <https://thefederalist.com/2023/07/15/if-you-were-a-sheep-during-covid-admit-you-were-wrong-and-do-better-next-time/>.

9. Carl R. Trueman, "Faithfulness Is the Future of the Church," *Religion & Liberty* 32.3, 5 July 2022 <https://www.acton.org/religion-liberty/volume-35-number-3/faithfulness-future-church>.

people experience forgiveness, but also numerical growth as the world sees communities where God is truly present and known by His people—a city on a hill cannot be hidden.

What does repentance look like, tangibly? This is a local, pastoral consideration. Some suggestions would be: services of lament and repentance; reaching out to members who have left the congregation and trying to make peace; public acknowledgements of mistakes and asking for collective and individual forgiveness. The goal should never be to rake leaders or laity over the coals, but to resolve to love one another in truth.

Some leaders might object that it is not possible or healthy to re-hash everything that happened during the pandemic. It is true that this must be done sensitively, not relitigating every decision. However, confession must be specific enough to be meaningful (not a mere cop-out, "mistakes were made"). To those who think that picking at this scab will do more harm than good, it should be pointed out that silence about sin leads to "wasting away" (Ps 32:3). Denial does not solve anything, but guarantees that future conflicts will lead to further fracture and pain. Instead, David says: "I acknowledged my sin to you, and I did not cover my iniquity; I said, 'I will confess my transgressions to YHWH,' and you forgave the iniquity of my sin" (Ps 32:5).

Furthermore, it is strategically wise to assess mistakes, repent of them, and plan for better decision-making in the future, during a time of relative *calm* rather than during the next crisis.

Practical Next Steps

If you are a lay person or a ruling elder, how might you begin a conversation concerning these issues with a pastor or other leaders? Every situation is different, but some general principles should be followed. First of all, any confrontation should be done respectfully, and gently, though firmly. I suspect that someone who has read this far and cares enough to confront a pastor on these issues may be harboring anger and hurt, as I have over these last several years. Make sure you search your heart in prayer before God, confessing any anger, prior to confronting a leader (Ps 139:23–24).

Pastors have a very difficult job in normal times, and during COVID many felt like they were in an impossible position between polarized opinions. Also, many pastors are older and were worried about their own risk from COVID.[10] Your aim should not be to rake them over the coals, or to make them sign on to some statement that they will never close their church again.[11] Rather, your encounter should be less confrontational, and more conversational. As we have seen in Ezekiel, God requires not complete perfection (otherwise, who could stand?), but directional repentance (Ezek 33:10–20). Exhort your pastor to reflect on the past—and to consider *now*, when the church is not in crisis, principles for handling the next crisis. This might not mean a list of specific practical measures that are and are not off the table. If there were another serious airborne virus but masks worked to protect against that virus, I would wear masks and encourage others to do so as well (and if they worked, people would not need to be coerced!). Rather, church leadership should be making a plan to biblically evaluate scientific claims and proposals, with a biblical view of scientific authorities, sphere sovereignty, and tradeoffs. Again, *now* is the time to think about principles—it is extremely difficult for leadership to formulate principles or maintain weakly-held principles in times of crisis.

---

10. Pastors should take note of the story of Saint Charles Borromeo, a sixteenth-century Archbishop of Milan, who risked his own life in attending to the spiritual and sacramental needs of his city during a Black Death outbreak: Domenick Galatolo, "Saint Charles Borromeo's Courageous Response to the Plague," *America Needs Fatima* blog, 21 April 2020 <https://www.americaneeds-fatima.org/blog/st-charles-borromeos-courageous-response-to-the-plague>.

11. Though, if they want to sign a statement, here is a good one: "The Frankfurt Declaration of Christian & Civil Liberties," August 2022 <https://frankfurtdeclaration.com>.

If you are a pastor or a church leader who has genuine regrets over your handling of COVID, what should you do? God somehow works through imperfect human authorities—honest leaders know this better than anyone. We should wake up each day keenly aware of our flaws and sins, and giving God glory for how his strength is shown to be perfect in our weaknesses (2 Cor 12:9). Confessing failure of leadership is not a flaw, but a strength. On the other hand, leadership requires courage of conviction. If we cannot handle any criticism or disapproval of those in our charge or outside our flock, then we should not be in leadership.

Some readers will ask, "What COVID leadership failures disqualify someone from leadership?" I prefer not to pontificate or prescribe specifics, but to leave this up to God and to the denominations and church courts to decide if unrepentance for leadership failures warrants removal from office. However, true repentance should be a requirement for staying in church leadership. I do think that the failures of closing church for extended periods of time, segregating congregations, and binding consciences are serious spiritual errors which must be repented of.

The church has historically faced crises of widespread compromise among authorities. In the survey of Ezekiel leadership texts (Chapter 11), I confess that I do not understand how in Ezekiel 44 the Levites are excoriated but the Zadoqites are exonerated. The Donatist controversy in the early fourth-century AD is another moment when leaders who had been unfaithful under persecution were reinstated as priests and bishops, to the dismay of those who had stood firm under persecution. The conclusion of the church catholic—that God works through the valid sacraments and ministry of even sinful or spiritually disqualified leaders—should give us comfort that the Holy Spirit will continue to work in Christ's imperfect church.

Acknowledging and repenting of COVID failures will lead to reconciliation and greater spread of the gospel. The "truth and reconciliation" model doesn't visit reprisals or impose "a reckoning" according to human vengeance (which is not godly: Rom 12:19; James 1:20). But reconciliation is only possible if the truth is accurately told.[12]

Re-Forming Beyond COVID

In considering how the church can be not only "reformed"—brought more closely into alignment with God's will revealed in the Bible—churches are faced with the opportunity to re-form—that is, to bring the members of the church back together in ways that might differ from the pre-COVID situation.

Mere simultaneity effected by technology, as we saw in Chapter 7, can actually accelerate the destruction of true community. One solution, then, is to re-instill the value of *unity* and *presence*, for which *mere simultaneity* has been a cheap substitute—even before COVID. The pandemic offers an opportunity to reform our worship according to scripture—we must resist the tendency to merely cope, while hoping to revert to a pre-COVID situation.

The local church should be re-formed around at least three essentials, which may be enacted in accordance with various Christian convictions and traditions. First, we are commanded to meet as the church, in local bodies, regularly (Heb 10:25). However, scripture does not guarantee that we will be able to meet just as we always have. The imperative to meet for worship does not require us to meet indoors for the sake of comfort or electronic equipment, or in large groups, or without masks and appropriate physical distance. But we "must not abandon the habit of meeting together," as scripture says.

12. Jay Bhattacharya and Martin Kulldorff, "The COVID Wars: Will America revert to lockdowns and panic again? Watch the debate taking place now," *Tablet*, 13 November 2023 <https://www.tabletmag.com/sections/news/articles/the-covid-wars>.

Second, local congregations might consider more frequent celebration of communion when meeting in person. We are corporeal beings; this embodied act is part of our fellowship with God and one another, and makes worship clearly distinct from electronically-mediated forms of supplemental fellowship (e.g., online prayer groups). If it is necessary to meet in smaller groups than we are accustomed to, it is better to celebrate the Lord's Supper in small home gatherings as unique, discrete celebrations—not virtually as part of a large online group, eating and drinking simultaneously.[13]

Third, the "fellowship of the saints" as a means of God's grace in our lives entails allowing myself to be *truly known* by others, and allowing those fellow believers (and ordained officers) to have authority in my life, holding me accountable to God's Word. This requires time, work, vulnerability, and time spent together—none of which is adequately facilitated by online presence or connection.

As I wrote at the conclusion of my 2019 article,[14] each of these elements of re-formed church looks different according to the theological tradition in which the church is situated. Each tradition has some strengths and some weaknesses that will surface during this time. However, I think we will find that some ecclesiologies are better-poised than others to weather this current storm. For example, Catholics and Reformed can appreciate the simplicity, flexibility, and locality of the Anabaptist tradition,

---

13. We have not even addressed the practices of foot-washing, which is regarded in some traditions (especially Pentecostal and Anabaptist churches) as an ordinance, and "greeting with a holy kiss," commanded four times in Paul's letters (Rom 16:16; 1 Cor 16:20; 2 Cor 13:12; 1 Thes 5:26). These practices might be evaluated for their "essentialness" or safety during a pandemic using the calculus outlined that includes both material and spiritual costs and benefits. But regardless of specific assessment, the very fact of these physical, non-discursive practices in the New Testament points to the essentialness of gathering physically together for worship as Christian family, united across lines of gender, class, race, and ethnicity.

14. Benjamin Giffone, "Technologising of Word and Sacrament: Deuteronomy 14:24–26 and Intermediation in Worship," *EJT* 28.1 (2019): 66–77.

which has long been receptive to house churches and small gatherings. Conversely, Anabaptists might learn from the stronger sacramental theology of the Reformed or Lutheran traditions, in which spiritual and physical presence are more intimately intertwined. Some traditions are inherently more amenable to borrowing the practices of other traditions—but a church may find that measures taken by local bodies in other traditions simply cannot be adopted without compromising key convictions.[15] Structural adaptations in our worship may necessitate the breakup of larger congregations into smaller bodies—and there will be gains (more intimate fellowship) and losses (less specialization in terms of ministries that can be offered).

Rather than *mere simultaneity* or the simple transfer of discursive information from God, biblical values that underpin our worship practice are: fidelity to God and his Word; hospitality; and discipleship. In exercising hospitality, we become disciples of the God who invites us to his table and serves us—think of the seventy elders of Israel who ate and drank with God (Exod 24:9–11), or of Jesus washing the disciples' feet and commanding them to do likewise (John 13:3–20). The church is to be hospitable, a haven for the weary, a Spirit-filled outpost of Christ's coming kingdom. All of these notions require physical presence. Yet hospitality also requires that we balance service with prudence, with proper precautions given all that we know about sanitation and the spread of disease.

In light of all these considerations, it is apparent to me that churches should move away from livestreaming services. While a livestream provides a small benefit to a handful of people, for others it will be a less-satisfying experience that prevents them from fully hungering for church fellowship (see Chapter 8). In the

---

15. Examples for consideration might be the role of the priesthood in the Eucharist within the Roman Catholic, Eastern Orthodox, and Anglican traditions; and the exercise of sign gifts—tongues, prophecy—in Pentecostal and charismatic churches.

"old days," those who missed a Sunday but really wanted to hear the sermon could request a recording (I remember when this was a cassette tape ministry!). Members who are homebound can still listen to recorded sermons. What if instead of putting volunteer energies into livestreaming (not to mention tithe money diverted to expensive equipment, software and subscriptions/hosting), a congregation dispatched deacons or members from the church to actually visit homebound members, bring them recordings (or show them how to download them), along with a greeting, a meal, a scripture, a prayer, a song?

It seems to me that every person who could potentially benefit from a livestream, would stand to benefit *more* from getting rid of the livestream and replacing it with embodied presence— either worshiping in church, or with regular visitation.

Each tradition needs to think critically before simply adopting practices from other traditions—and perhaps seek out and retrieve better alternatives from its own past. Moreover, churches should be extremely cautious about introducing technology into worship; it never *merely* replicates the old—it restructures into something new. If we choose to stick with a technology temporarily during a crisis, we must openly name and steadfastly resist its negative effects, and (preferably) go back to a biblical structure of worship as soon as possible.

CHAPTER 18 | Hope for Reconciliation and Restoration

I have tried very hard to imagine what various readers of this book who have reached the concluding chapter might be thinking and feeling. No doubt some will feel relieved to have had some of their concerns and troubles given voice. Others will feel angry and defensive, and will have disagreed strongly with many of the arguments I have made.

Anticipating this, I have considered carefully how to provide a conclusion that is both logically consistent and satisfying in relation to the rest of the book, and also pastorally appropriate for all readers in a range of emotions and degrees of disagreement.

I have decided that the best conclusion is to put forward some important relevant examples from the Bible, some of which "tie up loose ends" from examples of conflict and failure cited previously in this book. It is these examples, and the promises of the God who reveals himself, that give me hope for the church and for the world.

The questions running through this book are epistemological and teleological: how do we as humans *know*, and what *purpose* do we have? The answer is that the true God is knowable, and he has not left himself without continuing revelation *and* presence in this world: Word, sacrament, and the Spirit-filled church. Despite all of the spiritual darkness, the dead-end counternarratives of modernity, scientism and other ideologies, and coercion and censorship—God's truth wins out in the end.

Gospel Reconciliation Between Apostles

In Chapters 14 and 15, we noted that in Galatians 2:11–14 Paul rebuked several other Christian leaders, including Barnabas, his former missionary partner: James, the brother of Jesus and *primus inter pares* at the Jerusalem Council (Acts 15:13); and even Peter, one of the original apostles. Even though these men were leaders and had previously acted courageously and admirably in proclaiming the gospel and leading the church—on this issue, Paul corrected them publicly and forcefully, out of love and fidelity to the Savior who had called each of them.

An additional, less theologically significant rift had opened between Paul and Barnabas. They had separated following Paul's first missionary journey, over whether they should take Mark, Barnabas's cousin (cf. Col 4:10), who had left them during their previous journey (Acts 15:36–41).

There are no narratives in the New Testament that explicitly recount resolution, repentance, or reconciliation between Paul and these three leaders. Yet when we look to their letters to the churches, we find evidence. In his Second Letter, Peter refers to "our beloved brother Paul" and "the wisdom given him" presented to the church "in all his letters" (2 Pet 3:15–16). Peter maintained a high regard for Paul, calling him "brother," and acknowledging revealed "wisdom" in Paul's writings. It is not a stretch to regard this as evidence that Peter had received Paul's Galatians 2 rebuke in a humble spirit and corrected course—exactly what Paul had hoped would happen.

Mark and Paul apparently later reconciled, and resumed ministry together. Paul refers to Mark three times in his letters. He indicates that Mark visits and attends to him in his imprisonment

(Col 4:10); he calls Mark "a fellow worker" (Phlm 24) and "very useful to me in my ministry" (2 Tim 4:11). We may speculate that, since Barnabas's loyalty to his cousin was a cause of his falling-out with Paul, Paul and Barnabas might subsequently have reconciled, also.[1]

Sharp disagreement among Christian leaders arose in the early church, as it has arisen many times since, and most recently, amidst the COVID crisis. Disagreement, rebuke, and correction are part of the process by which the Holy Spirit refines and sanctifies Christ's church and individuals within it. Even though I have presented some harsh criticism and painted a dark picture of the temporal realities we face, I remain hopeful because Christ is risen and has sent the Spirit to finish that mission of sanctification.

The Gospel According to Ezekiel

I have heard the COVID crisis aptly described as an *apocalypse*, in the technical sense of a *revelation* or *unveiling* of what was already true of the temporal world, institutions, and individuals prior to the crisis. In biblical apocalyptic literature, the curtain of the visible realm is pulled back, so that a prophet receiving the vision can see the underlying spiritual realities.

Those underlying realities are usually not pleasant, at least at the beginning of the vision (usually the prophet's own "present"). Underlying corrupt realities are difficult to accept—we would rather keep the veneer of stability and health.

But unveiling allows corruption to be acknowledged and repented of, evil to be defeated, and sickness to be healed. That is the divine hope that is the conclusion of apocalypse.

---

1. James R. Wood, "Sheep, Wolves, and Fools: On the Perils of a Winsome Ministry," *American Reformer*, 4 October 2022 <https://americanreformer.org/2022/10/sheep-wolves-and-fools/>.

Ezekiel is one of the biblical books with strong apocalyptic elements (Daniel 7–12 and Revelation being the "full-blown" canonical apocalypses). In Chapter 11 of this book, we saw that in Ezekiel 8–9 the "curtain" hiding the spiritual corruption of leadership was "drawn back" in Ezekiel's vision. But we also saw in Ezekiel's visions of the future: a Good Shepherd (Ezek 34), new hearts for the people, including the leaders (Ezek 36), and reinstated leadership (Ezek 44).

Despite the harsh condemnation in the book of Ezekiel for leaders and institutions that fail, Ezekiel also contains great hope for all God's people, because of God's own power, character, and actions for the sake of his own glory.

Ezekiel 1 begins with the terrifying vision of God's holiness that causes Ezekiel to fall on his face (1:28). The glory and holiness of the Triune God should be constantly before us, and promoting his glory should be our chief purpose as leaders, as Christians, and as human beings. We consistently fall short of God's glory due to our sin—Ezekiel is sent on a mission to tell both the Israelites (2:1–7) and the nations (25–32) their sinfulness. Yet the final section of the book, chapters 40–48, reminds us of God's goal of fellowship with his people; the book concludes, "And the name of the city from that time on shall be, YHWH Is There" (48:35b).

Therefore, despite all of the sins and rebellion of his people chronicled in chapters 16, 20, and 23, God is radically gracious. He will make his people holy, whether we like it or not (20:32–44), so he can receive glory ("for the sake of My name"), and so that he can have fellowship with us. On that journey of sanctification (individual and corporate), we can be confident that God is present with us, even when he harshly disciplines his people:

> Therefore say, 'Thus says the Lord GOD: Though I removed them far off among the nations, and though I scattered them among the countries, yet **I have been a**

sanctuary to them for a while in the countries where they have gone.' Therefore say, 'Thus says the Lord GOD: I will gather you from the peoples and assemble you out of the countries where you have been scattered, and I will give you the land of Israel.' And when they come there, they will remove from it all its detestable things and all its abominations. And I will give them one heart, and a new spirit I will put within them. I will remove the heart of stone from their flesh and give them a heart of flesh, that they may walk in my statutes and keep my rules and obey them. And they shall be my people, and I will be their God. (11:16–20, emphasis added)

Conclusion: Online Communion?

Let me return to the personal story I started with in Chapter 2: my dilemma over online communion back in April 2020. My Reformed view of communion as a sacrament made me uncomfortable about celebrating only with my family, in my home, apart from the body of Christ assembled for worship (even though I myself am an ordained minister). Ultimately, it was my view of the church and my commitment to our local (Anabaptist!) community that led me to celebrate online, simultaneously with others in our church thus "assembled," in good conscience.

Thankfully for my conscience, others in the church also discerned that this practice was simply not the same as celebrating communion in person, and so we did not continue with "online communion"—only live-streaming sermon, songs, and scripture readings for those few weeks. Thankfully for us in Lithuania, we were able to resume meeting in person only five weeks later, and celebrated the Lord's Supper together—in a larger room, with masks, using alcoholic wine (not our usual choice, due to pastoral concerns surrounding alcoholism), and disposable cups (we usually drank from a common cup). Despite the subdued atmosphere, and the absence of some at-risk folks who chose to stay home, it was a joyful reunion.

Those at-risk folks later returned to us for corporate worship, one-by-one. But even before their return, some of my most joyful experiences in ministry consisted of in-home visits to these brothers and sisters, to celebrate communion with them and the other pastor, sometimes in two languages. Even though home gatherings were forbidden by civil authorities, visits to perform "essential services" were allowed—and our church leadership decided that partaking in the body and blood of Christ is an essential act.

God has not left us without his Spirit, and he promises to be with us when we gather together. Our worship may look different depending on circumstances and conditions, but it can still be biblically faithful in its elements, and in the sincerity and fidelity of spirit among those who worship (John 4:23–24). Many of us live in cultures—modern secular Europe or North America—which do not accept in principle any limits to the scientific worldview to explain the world or engineer our way out of problems. We see the crisis of public confidence in these social and political institutions, which preceded the pandemic. The Christian church—in wisdom—must offer an alternative to modernity and scientism that is reasonable but *also joyful and deeply satisfying*: by marking ourselves out as "people of praise" (Joel 2:26–27), those whose lives are structured around corporate worship of the Triune God, whose orientation is toward Him and His kingdom.

SELECTED BIBLIOGRAPHY

As explained at the end of Chapter 1: for clarity of presentation, ephemeral sources (news reports, commentary/editorials, social media artifacts) are included in footnotes only, not relisted below.

Philosophical, Theological, and Social-Scientific Sources

Atlas, Scott W. *A Plague Upon Our House: My Fight at the Trump White House to Stop COVID from Destroying America.* Bombardier Books, 2021.

Berenson, Alex. *Pandemia: How Coronavirus Hysteria Took Over Our Government, Rights, and Lives.* Regnery, 2021.

Burridge, Richard A. *Holy Communion in Contagious Times: Celebrating the Eucharist in the Everyday and Online Worlds.* Eugene, OR: Cascade Books, 2022.

Callaham, Scott N. "Scripture and Worship." Pages 45–60 in *Dei Verbum: The Bible in Church and Society.* Singapore: The Ethos Institute for Public Christianity, 2020.

Caplan, Bryan. *The Myth of the Rational Voter: Why Democracies Choose Bad Policies.* Princeton: Princeton University Press, 2006.

Chan, Alina and Matthew Ridley. *Viral: The Search for the Origin of COVID-19.* New York: Harper, 2021.

Collins, Francis S. *The Road to Wisdom: On Truth, Science, Faith, and Trust.* New York: Little, Brown and Company & Worthy Books, 2024.

Conrad, Peter. *The Medicalization of Society: On the Transformation of Human Conditions into Treatable Disorders.* Baltimore: Johns Hopkins University Press, 2007.

Desmet, Mattias. *The Psychology of Totalitarianism*. Translated by Els VanBrabant. White River Junction, VT: Chelsea Green Publishing, 2022.

Douglas, Mary. "Atonement in Leviticus." *JSQ* 1.2 (1993/94): 109–130.

Douglas, Mary. *Leviticus as Literature*. Oxford: Oxford University Press, 2000.

Dreher, Rod. *Live Not By Lies: A Manual for Christian Dissidents*. New York: Sentinel, 2020.

Edwards, Aaron. "The Perennial Urgency of Theological Education," *EJT* 30.1 (2021): 167–190. DOI: 10.5117/EJT2021.1.009.EDWA.

Ellul, Jacques. *Propaganda: The Formation of Men's Attitudes*. Translated by Konrad Kellen and Jean Lerner. New York: Vintage Books, 1973 [1965].

Foster, Gigi, Paul Frijters and Michael Baker. *The Great Covid Panic: What Happened, Why, and What to Do Next*. Austin, TX: Brownstone Institute, 2021.

Giffone, Benjamin D. "'Anger Exhausted' for the Sake of YHWH's Name in Ezekiel 20: Did YHWH Really Relent from Wrath Poured Out on Israel?" *BZ* 66.1 (2022): 1–15.

Giffone, Benjamin D. "Atonement, Sacred Space and Ritual Time: The Chronicler as Reader of Priestly Pentateuchal Narrative." Pages 221–243 in *Chronicles and the Priestly Literature of the Hebrew Bible*. Edited by Louis Jonker and Jaeyoung Jeon. BZAW 528. Berlin: de Gruyter, 2021.

Giffone, Benjamin D. *My Salvation Is Close At Hand: Isaiah 56–66 for the Church After Christendom*. Eugene, OR: Wipf & Stock, 2025.

Giffone, Benjamin D. *Storymaking, Textual Development, and Varying Cultic Centralizations: Gathering and Fitting Unhewn Stones*. FAT II 142. Tübingen: Mohr Siebeck, 2023.

Giffone, Benjamin D. "Technologising of Word and Sacrament: Deuteronomy 14:24–26 and Intermediation in Worship." *EJT* 28.1 (2019): 66–77.

Gunton, Colin. *The One, the Three and the Many: God, Creation and the Culture of Modernity*. Cambridge: Cambridge University Press, 1993.

Gurri, Martin. *The Revolt of the Public and the Crisis of Authority in the New Millennium*. 2nd revised edition. San Francisco: Stripe Press, 2018 [2014].

Haidt, Jonathan. *The Anxious Generation: How the Great Rewiring of Childhood Is Causing an Epidemic of Mental Illness*. New York: Penguin Press, 2024.

Hayek, F.A. "The Pretence of Knowledge," Nobel lecture, 11 December 1974 <https://www.nobelprize.org/prizes/economic-sciences/1974/hayek/lecture/>.

Hayek, F.A. *The Fatal Conceit: The Errors of Socialism*. Edited by W.W. Bartley III. Chicago: University of Chicago Press, 1988.

Heiser, Michael S. *The Unseen Realm: Recovering the Supernatural Worldview of the Bible*. Bellingham, WA: Lexham, 2015.

Henderson, David R. "Daniel Kahneman." *Concise Encyclopedia of Economics*, n.d. <https://www.econlib.org/library/Enc/bios/Kahneman.html>.

Herman, Edward S. and Noam Chomsky. *Manufacturing Consent: The Political Economy of the Mass Media*. 2nd revised edition. New York: Pantheon Books, 2002 [1988].

Holcombe, Randall G. *Following Their Leaders: Political Preferences and Public Policy*. Cambridge Studies in Economics, Choice, and Society. New York: Cambridge University Press, 2023.

Horsley, Richard A., ed. *Paul and Empire: Religion and Power in Roman Imperial Society*. Harrisburg, PA: Trinity Press, International, 1997.

Jeon, Jaeyoung. "The Levites and Idolatry: A Scribal Debate in Ezekiel 44 and Chronicles." Pages 348–374 in *Chronicles and the Priestly Literature of the Hebrew Bible*. Edited by Louis Jonker and Jaeyoung Jeon. BZAW 528. Berlin: de Gruyter, 2021.

Johnson, Dru. *Knowledge By Ritual: A Biblical Prolegomenon to Sacramental Theology*. JTISupp 13. Winona Lake, IN: Eisenbrauns, 2016.

Kalpokas, Ignas. *Algorithmic Governance: Politics and Law in the Post-Human Era*. Cham, Switzerland: Palgrave Pivot, 2019.

Kilchör, Benjamin. "The Meaning of Ezekiel 44,6–14 in Light of Ezekiel 1–39." *Biblica* 98.2 (2017): 191–207.

Knight, Frank. *Freedom and Reform: Essays in Economics and Social Philosophy*. New York: Harper & Brothers, 1947.

Kuhn, Thomas S. *The Structure of Scientific Revolutions*. Chicago: University of Chicago Press, 1962.

MacDonald, Nathan. *Priestly Rule: Polemic and Biblical Interpretation in Ezekiel 44*. BZAW 476. Berlin: de Gruyter, 2015.

Middleton, J. Richard. *The Liberating Image: The Imago Dei in Genesis 1.* Grand Rapids, MI: Brazos Press, 2005.

Munger, Michael C. "Euvoluntary or Not, Exchange Is Just." *Social Philosophy and Policy* 28.2 (2011): 192–211. DOI: 10.1017/ S0265052510000269.

Noll, Mark. *The Scandal of the Evangelical Mind.* Grand Rapids: Eerdmans, 1994.

Ong, Walter S. *Orality and Literacy: The Technologizing of the Word. 30th Anniversary Edition: With Additional Chapters by John Hartley.* New York: Routledge, 2012 [1982].

Piper, John. *Coronavirus and Christ.* Wheaton, IL: Crossway, 2020.

Piper, John. *Let the Nations Be Glad! The Supremacy of God in Missions.* Grand Rapids, MI: Baker Books, 1993.

Polanyi, Michael. *Personal Knowledge: Towards a Post-Critical Philosophy.* Chicago: University of Chicago Press, 1974.

Price, S. R. F. "Rituals and Power." Pages 47–71 in *Paul and Empire: Religion and Power in Roman Imperial Society.* Edited by Richard A. Horsley. Harrisburg, PA: Trinity Press, International, 1997.

Price, S. R. F. *Rituals and Power: The Roman Imperial Cult in Asia Minor.* Cambridge: Cambridge University Press, 1984.

Putnam, Robert D. *Bowling Alone: The Collapse and Revival of American Community.* New York: Simon & Schuster, 2000.

Ricoeur, Paul. *Memory, History, Forgetting.* Translated by Kathleen Blamey and David Pellauer. Chicago: University of Chicago Press, 2004.

Schnittjer, Gary E. *The Torah Story: An Apprenticeship on the Pentateuch.* Grand Rapids: Zondervan, 2006.

Scott, John and Gordon Marshall, eds. "Social Distance." Page 700 in *A Dictionary of Sociology*, 3rd edition. New York: Oxford University Press, 2009.

Sedláček, Tomáš. *Economics of Good and Evil: The Quest for Economic Meaning from Gilgamesh to Wall Street.* Oxford: Oxford University Press, 2011.

Siker, Jeffrey S. *Liquid Scripture: The Bible in a Digital World.* Minneapolis: Fortress, 2017.

Smith, James K. A. *You Are What You Love.* Grand Rapids: Brazos Press, 2016.

Somin, Ilya, with Kevin L. Cope and Alexander Stremitzer. "Vaccine Passports as a Constitutional Right." *Arizona State Law Journal* 51 (2022) <https://papers.ssrn.com/sol3/papers.cfm?abstract_id=3910194>.

Stenschke, Christoph. "The 'Strong' and the 'Weak' in Romans 14:1–15:13 and Covid-19-Related Tensions in Christian Congregations: The Prospects and Perils of Relating Current Concerns to Sacred Scripture." *Neotestamentica* 57.1 (2023): 25–56.

Taylor, Charles. *A Secular Age.* Cambridge, MA: Belknap Press of Harvard University Press, 2007.

Trueman, Carl R. "Faithfulness Is the Future of the Church." *Religion & Liberty* 32.3 (July 2022). <https://www.acton.org/religion-liberty/volume-35-number-3/faithfulness-future-church>.

Walker, Andrew T. "The Wax Nose of Neighbor Love." *Public Discourse*, 15 April 2024 <https://www.thepublicdiscourse.com/2024/04/93212/>.

Woods, Thomas E., Jr. *Collateral Damage: Victims of the Lockdown Regime Tell Their Stories.* eBook, 2023.

Woods, Thomas E., Jr. *Diary of a Psychosis: How Public Health Disgraced Itself During COVID Mania.* Libertarian Institute, 2023.

Wright, N.T. *God and the Pandemic: A Christian Reflection on the Coronavirus and Its Aftermath.* Grand Rapids, MI: Zondervan, 2020.

Wright, N. T. *History and Eschatology: Jesus and the Promise of Natural Theology.* London: SPCK, 2019.

Wright, N. T. *Surprised By Hope: Rethinking Heaven, the Resurrection, and the Mission of the Church.* New York: HarperOne, 2008.

Wright, N. T. *The Resurrection of the Son of God.* Minneapolis: Fortress Press, 2003.

Wright, N.T. *Paul and the Faithfulness of God.* Minneapolis: Fortress, 2013.

Natural/Medical Science Journal Articles

"Human Experimentation: Code Of Ethics Of The World Medical Association—Declaration Of Helsinki," *British Medical Journal* 1964;2(5402):177 <https://doi.org/10.1136/bmj.2.5402.177>.

Bardosh, Kevin et al. "The Unintended Consequences Of COVID-19 Vaccine Policy: Why Mandates, Passports And Restrictions May

Cause More Harm Than Good." *BMJ Global Health* 2022;7:e008684 <https://doi.org/10.1136/bmjgh-2022-008684>.

Block, Jennifer. "Vaccinating People Who Have Had Covid-19: Why Doesn't Natural Immunity Count In The US?" *BMJ* 2021; 374 :n2101 doi:10.1136/bmj.n2101 <https://doi.org/10.1136/bmj.n2101>.

Cao, S., Gan, Y., Wang, C. et al. "Post-lockdown SARS-CoV-2 nucleic acid screening in nearly ten million residents of Wuhan, China." *Nat Commun* 11, 5917 (2020), <https://doi.org/10.1038/s41467-020-19802-w>.

Crump, Andy. "Ivermectin: Enigmatic Multifaceted 'Wonder' Drug Continues To Surprise And Exceed Expectations." *Journal of Antibiotics* 70 (2017): 495–505 <https://doi.org/10.1038/ja.2017.11>.

Doshi, Peter. "Covid-19: Researchers Face Wait For Patient Level Data From Pfizer And Moderna Vaccine Trials." *BMJ* 2022; 378 doi: https://doi.org/10.1136/bmj.o1731 (Published 12 July 2022).

Epperly, David E., Kristopher R. Rinehart, David N. Caney. "COVID-19 Aerosolized Viral Loads, Environment, Ventilation, Masks, Exposure Time, Severity, And Immune Response: A Pragmatic Guide Of Estimates." medRxiv 2020.10.03.20206110; doi: https://doi.org/10.1101/2020.10.03.20206110

Fraiman, Joseph et al. "Serious Adverse Events Of Special Interest Following Mrna COVID-19 Vaccination In Randomized Trials In Adults." *Vaccine* 40:40 (22 September 2022), 5798–5805 <https://doi.org/10.1016/j.vaccine.2022.08.036>.

Hall, V. et al. "Do Antibody Positive Healthcare Workers Have Lower SARS-Cov-2 Infection Rates Than Antibody Negative Healthcare Workers? Large Multi-Centre Prospective Cohort Study (The SIREN Study), England: June To November 2020." medRxiv 2021.01.13.21249642; doi: https://doi.org/10.1101/2021.01.13.21249642.

Ioannidis, John P. A. et al. "Age-Stratified Infection Fatality Rate Of COVID-19 In The Non-Elderly Population." *Environmental research* 216 (Pt 3), 114655 <https://doi.org/10.1016/j.envres.2022.114655>.

Ioannidis, John P. A. "Why Most Published Research Findings Are False." PLoS Med. 2005 Aug 30;2(8):e124 <https://doi.org/10.1371/journal.pmed.0020124>.

Klompas, M. et al. "Perspective: Universal Masking in Hospitals in the Covid-19 Era," *New England Journal of Medicine* 382.63 (May 2020) <https://www.nejm.org/doi/full/10.1056/NEJMp2006372>.

Liu, Ian T., Vinay Prasad and Jonathan J. Darrow. "How Effective Are Cloth Face Masks? A Summary Of The Scientific Literature On The Effectiveness Of Masking, Both Against Respiratory Infection Generally And Against COVID-19." *Regulation,* Winter 2021/2022 <https://www.cato.org/regulation/winter-2021/2022/how-effective-are-cloth-face-masks>.

Malhotra, Aseem. "Curing the pandemic of misinformation on COVID-19 mRNA vaccines through real evidence-based medicine - Part 2." *Journal of Metabolic Health* [Online] 5.1 (26 September 2022) <http://dx.doi.org/10.7759/cureus.57960>.

Massetti, G.M. et al. "Summary of Guidance for Minimizing the Impact of COVID-19 on Individual Persons, Communities, and Health Care Systems—United States, August 2022." *MMWR Morb Mortal Wkly Rep* 2022;71:1057-1064. DOI: http://dx.doi.org/10.15585/mmwr.mm7133e1

Rothwell, Jonathan T., Alexandru Cojocaru, Rajesh Srinivasan and Yeon Soo Kim. "Global Evidence On The Economic Effects Of Disease Suppression During COVID-19," *Humanities & Social Sciences Communications* (2024)11:78, <https://doi.org/10.1057/s41599-023-02571-4>.

Smith, Richard. "Time to assume that health research is fraudulent until proven otherwise?" *BMJ Opinion*, 5 July 2021 <https://blogs.bmj.com/bmj/2021/07/05/time-to-assume-that-health-research-is-fraudulent-until-proved-otherwise/>.

Thacker, Paul D. "Covid-19: Researcher Blows The Whistle On Data Integrity Issues In Pfizer's Vaccine Trial." *BMJ* 2021; 375 :n2635 doi:10.1136/bmj.n2635.

INDEX

Hebrew Bible

New Testament

Subjects

Made in United States
Cleveland, OH
17 June 2025

17782184R10141